My Search in ....

for

The Secret Wish-Fulfilling Jewel

by

Peter Mt. Shasta

Published by Church of the Seven Rays

Copyright 2016 by Peter Mt. Shasta

ISBN: 978-0998414317

Cover art: "Himalayas" by Nicholas Roerich, 1933; with the permission of the Roerich Museum, New York. Cover design: Susanne Meyer.

Other books by Peter Mt. Shasta:

"I AM" the Open Door

"I AM" Affirmations and the Secret of their Effective Use

Search for the Guru: Adventures of a Western Mystic, Book I

Apprentice to the Masters: Adventures of a Western Mystic, Book II

Lady Master Pearl, My Teacher

I AM the Living Christ

Also available as eBooks through the author's website:
www.i-am-teachings.com

Reviews

Couldn't stop reading it!! Thank You, Thank You, so much for sharing your experiences in Tibet and reminding us of how we are one, and our thoughts are so powerful. Demons manifested by our thoughts may take lifetimes to be dissolved, and only love can do that.

-Pratibha Dayal, Mumbai, India

I spent years studying Tibetan Buddhism and learned more from this book than I ever learned in all the empowerments that I did and retreats that I went on. . . . It also made me feel like I threw the baby out with the bathwater, as they say . . . so this is very helpful for me. Of course, I am a big devotee of the Dalai Lama. Thank you for sharing this. I am sure Saint Germain is very pleased

–Donna Gaus, Ecuador

You have written several incredible books. I believe many millions will get to know your rich, worldly, and spiritual experiences from those books. I hope they will bring positive spiritual development and happiness to the reader.

–Tenzin Topgyal, General Secretary
Institute of Buddhist Dialectics
Dharamsala, India

TABLE OF CONTENTS

Appreciation

I would like to thank Yemana Sanders for her inspiration and encouragement during the writing of this book. Many thanks also to those who helped with the editing, especially Donna Guas, Tjalling Heyning, Daye Proffit, Julie Wolfe, and Sara Zimmerman, all of whom made valuable contributions for which I am grateful. I would also like to express my appreciation to Susanne Meyer for her assistance with the cover design and the translation into German. Sincere thanks also to Reinhold Köglmeier for assisting with the German translation.

Preface

I introduced a portion of the Ancient Wisdom to the western world in the 1930s through Guy Ballard, who wrote under the name Godfre Ray King. As this was a time of economic and moral crisis in the West known as the Great Depression, it was hoped by the other Masters and myself that these teachings on the inner God Presence would help raise individuals out of their sense of victimhood and empower them with the ability to change their relationship to life. These teachings were not intended as the final teachings on the spiritual path, but the first part of a gradual revelation to the West of the ancient wisdom long known in the Far East.

I now wish that further teachings be revealed, devoid of the religious and cultural associations with which they are found in India, Tibet, and China, so I am now inspiring Peter Mt. Shasta to reveal some of those teachings here. Please keep in mind that no words can convey the ultimate truth, which can only be experienced within.

-Saint Germain

July 4, 2016
Jade Lake, East Meredith, NY

Note

This book is based on my personal journeys to the East, specifically Tibet and Dharamsala, India. Certain time sequences have been compressed to eliminate mundane events, and names have been changed to preserve privacy.

Many years have elapsed since the experiences written about here, and although I have endeavored to incorporate all I learned into my subsequent books and talks, I have only now ventured to write this partial account of this particular journey. The impetus to write came during a retreat in a cabin in the mountains of upstate New York, when Saint Germain reminded me of what I had previously agreed to accomplish.

Chintamani Mahakala reveals secrets of Buddhist alchemy: that genuine wealth is achieved through generosity.... Giving away all we achieve—mentally, spiritually, and materially—we are born anew in the Buddha field of vast abundance, free of avarice and fear.... The emanations of the mind's deepest dimensions may at first seem horrific, but recognized as unexplored regions of the psyche, they offer complete liberation from our slavery to emotional and material attachments...."
-Ian A. Baker, *Celestial Gallery* (Callaway, 2000).

Sixteenth Karmapa

Chapter 1

Call to Tibet

One of my ancestors was the first westerner to enter Tibet, or so my grandmother said. After seeing the death and suffering of the Civil War, her grandfather had journeyed to that legendary kingdom— most likely to seek refuge from the prevailing chaos.[1] As a child, the story made such an impact that I wished I could someday journey to that peaceful place known then as the roof of the world. Had his search for truth in the eighteen hundreds imprinted itself on our family destiny, and so shaped my own future?

On my first journey to India in 1971, that wish was almost fulfilled. Wandering in the mountains near the Tibetan border, I met a fellow American on the trail who spoke of a magical Wish-Fulfilling Jewel that existed in Tibet. It was rumored to cure physical and emotional problems, but above all to grant the fulfillment of wishes. I thought of hiking over the pass into that forbidden land to seek that jewel, but when I heard that the Communists were shooting anyone they found in the pass, I postponed the quest.

I returned home to New York and then drove westward to California, but as I stayed with a friend in Berkeley, I found that the pursuit of sensory desires and the acquisition of material things no longer interested me. I longed for the higher worlds I had experienced in meditation in the Himalayas. I thought of the yogi I had lived with in the Kumon Hills who, under the

---

[1] Other westerners also supposedly entered Tibet in the nineteenth century.

instruction of the great Babaji, was preparing to leave his body. I longed to do the same.

Early one morning I drove across the Golden Gate Bridge to Muir Woods, where I hoped to end my earthly life, but it was then that the Master known as Saint Germain appeared, materializing out of the air in physical form. He offered liberation, but after he opened my eyes to the suffering of the world, I felt such compassion that I no longer wanted to leave. He said that as I had chosen to stay, he was sending me to Mount Shasta to receive training that would enable me to assist him in his work for humanity. There I was trained by Pearl Dorris, former assistant to Godfre Ray King, in how to contact the I AM Presence and invoke its God power in everyday life (Read the full account in my autobiography, *Apprentice to the Masters: Adventures of a Western Mystic, Book II).*[2]

As part of my training and service, I was subsequently sent to Lake Titicaca, the Great Pyramid, and back to visit Sathya Sai Baba in India. By then, I had exhausted my finances and was living in a small apartment in Mount Shasta. The following adventure began in 1997.

Early one morning I was meditating when, to my great surprise, the Sixteenth Karmapa appeared overhead. He had left his physical body thirteen years before, yet now his radiance was unmistakable, raising

---

2 Godfre Ray King, born Guy Ballard, author of *Unveiled Mysteries, The Magic Presence,* and *I AM Discourses;* also founder of the Saint Germain Foundation. My biography of Pearl is *Lady Master Pearl, My Teacher* (Church of the Seven Rays, 2015)

me in consciousness.[3] Since I never prayed to this being, I was surprised at his sudden appearance, and even more surprised when he said, "I want you to go to Tibet."

"What?" I retorted, thinking that I might be imagining.

"Go to Tibet," he repeated.

"Why?" I asked, a question I have since learned the Masters rarely answer.

"Visit the new Karmapa."

Since I was now conversing with the Karmapa, I did not see the point in going half way around the world to see his new form.

"That's it?" I asked.

"Also, seek that for which you have long wished," he said, after a moment's pause.

"What is that?"

"The Precious Wish-Fulfilling Jewel."

"But, I don't have enough money to go to Tibet."

He laughed, and disappeared.

I had experienced over the years that the Masters would frequently push me to spend every last cent, so over the past couple of years whenever I managed to save a little money I had begun stashing it in a hidden pocket in my suitcase in the back of the closet, hoping the Masters would not notice. Was I now going to have to draw on this? In the long run I realized that seeming impediments such as lack of money mean little to the Great Ones; when they want you to do something, the way opens and the means are provided. None-the-less,

---

[3] The Sixteenth Karmapa, Rangjung Rigpe Dorje, was regarded by the Tibetans as a living Buddha. He left his body in 1981, thirteen years prior to this appearance.

I liked to feel that I had at least the illusion of financial security.

Am I really meant to go to Tibet, or is this yet another test, I wondered? I meditated on my Higher Self, the I AM Presence, and also sent a telepathic message to my mentor, the Master Saint Germain, for confirmation. I vowed that I would only go if I received a personal invitation from the Dalai Lama. Since I was sure that he didn't have my phone number, an invitation from him didn't seem likely.

I decided to say affirmations to clear my mind and create the intention to receive guidance. I had discovered that the words following the statement I AM invoke the Source and alter one's consciousness, but only when repeated in stillness and oneness with the Source. Otherwise, repeating affirmations simply strengthens the ego and personal will.

I affirmed,

> *I AM free of all wrong thoughts and desires,*
> *and I AM filled with the desire to do only*
> *what is according to the Divine Plan.*

The next day I began investigating travel options. Getting to Tibet would require much planning and a substantial sum of money. It was the early days of the Internet, and I had only a slow dial-up connection. I sent out a few requests for information to travel agents and received a few emails, but no invitation from the Dalai Lama.

However, a few days later the phone rang and I was surprised to hear a girl ask, "Is this Peter?"

"Yes."

"I understand that you would like to go to Tibet?"

"How did you hear that?"

"Someone forwarded me your email."

"Well, I've been thinking about Tibet, but will only go if I'm invited by the Dalai Lama."

"The Dalai Lama happens to be my uncle, and I'm inviting you. Is that good enough?"

"What! The Dalai Lama is your uncle?"

"Yes, my father is His Holiness' brother. He came to the US a long time ago, and I'm his daughter. I work for a travel agency in Colorado."

I was shocked. "Well, I'm also not sure I can afford the trip. What does it cost?"

The price she quoted was exactly the amount I had saved in my secret stash to the very dollar. I mumbled I would think about it.

That night I rose to use the bathroom, and when I flipped on the light, there was the Dalai Lama standing there, as clear as day. Before I could say anything, he said, "I have something for you to do."

"What's that?" I blurted, still in shock, but he was gone. Although I knew he had visited in his etheric body, his form was as clear as if physical. I stayed awake for hours, wondering why he had appeared and what he wanted me to do. I meditated on the affirmation:

> *I AM the Illumining, Revealing Presence,*
> *showing what I am meant to know,*
> *and doing what I am meant to do.*

By morning I had not received any direct message. Whenever I needed help, I never prayed to beings on the physical plane, but instead to the Ascended Masters, for I knew that as long as someone is still human, there is the possibility of error. So, who were these Tibetans that were now appearing, and should I follow their requests? First there was the Karmapa, and now the Dalai Lama? I knew that Saint Germain would not allow this contact if it were not part of some plan, but what plan? Perhaps it was a test? Although there was no verbal message, I did feel an urge to return the phone call to the Dalai Lama's niece and take the reservation she had offered. When I told her that her uncle had appeared to me during the night and made a request, she laughed. "I guess he didn't need your phone number."

After I hung up, I paced the room. At last I was going to fulfill my childhood wish! I wondered what the Dalai Lama wanted, and if it would lead to the Wish-Fulfilling Jewel.

I was leaving in two weeks and began to gather the warm clothes I would need. Then, one night I had a terrifying experience that made me fear going to Tibet. I awakened to an ominous presence in the room, and as I looked up, I saw a demonic being. Fangs protruded from his open mouth, and on his head was a crown of five human skulls. It shouted, "I will never let you enter Tibet," and disappeared.

Fearful about going back to sleep, I sat up and wondered if it was too late to cancel the trip and get a refund. I had read stories of the demons that used to inhabit Tibet, and had no desire to risk being possessed.

Supposedly the Indian *mahasiddha*, Padmasambhava, who had brought tantric Buddhism to Tibet in the eighth century, had subdued these beings and forced them to act as protectors of the Buddha Dharma.[4] However, it seemed that one of them had escaped.

The next night before going to bed, I prayed for protection and enfolded myself in the Crystal Cloak of Mighty Victory.[5] With great determination I said,

I AM invincibly protected by the Crystal Cloak of Mighty Victory.

I call on Archangel Michael, Saint Germain, and all other Ascended Masters, to protect me at all times, by the Power of God That I AM!

The Light of God Never Fails, The Light of God Never Fails, The Light of God Never Fails, and I AM That Light!

---

[4] *Mahasiddha* (English: Master), one who has achieved great perfection and power. There are varying degrees of mastery; generally in this text I use the term Master to refer to the Ascended Masters, who no longer dwell on the physical plane. Ascension is called *jalus* in Tibetan, the attainment of the Rainbow Body.

[5] The Crystal Cloak of Mighty Victory is a visualization that can be employed as a tantric practice. One first enters into a state of meditative absorption, and then visualizes the being known as Might Victory, a being who has never known defeat, clothed in a cloak of crystal. That being then dissolves into light and merges with oneself. One is then clothed with the crystal cloak and is invincibly protected.

Even though I knew that the Masters would not allow any ultimate harm to befall one of their students, I knew that it was up to me to dissolve the fear. Finally, I fell asleep, but during the night was awakened again by someone in the room. This time the presence was friendly, that of a woman I'd known for years, but who had died six months before. Although only in her fifties and in almost perfect health, one day she collapsed while walking across the room. She had been a long-time student of the Masters, and I had asked the Masters to clear her of any remaining karma and to raise her into the Ascended state. She had been a powerful woman with a strong inner light, and now she spoke with an even greater power, "That being will not bother you again!" With that, she disappeared.

After three days of travel on multiple flights and a layover in Bangkok, I finally arrived exhausted in Kathmandu. I hoped that a representative of the hotel where the tour had made a reservation would greet me, but when I looked out at the sea of faces and the placards held aloft by various hotel shuttles and tour operators, I could not see any welcoming sign. At baggage claim I stood staring at the conveyer belt for half an hour until I realized my duffel bag had not arrived. The bag full of warm clothes and supplements to help in acclimatizing to the altitude was probably on a carousel in one of the airports between Seattle and Bangkok. I talked to an airport official who looked up, annoyed, and asked me fill out a form.

"Don't worry, it will be on the next flight," he said.
"When is that?"
"Tomorrow, same time."

"But, I'm flying to Lhasa tomorrow morning," I stammered.

"Tough luck; maybe it will be here when you get back."

I slung my backpack over my shoulder and staggered outside into the moist heat. The moment I reached the sidewalk I was besieged by several boys, each tugging me in a different direction and shouting the names of competing enterprises, "Snowlands Hotel? Trek Tours? Snow Lion Tours?"

"No. Shambhala!" I shouted, fighting to hold on to my backpack, but it was no use. One of them snatched it and took off through the crowd. When I caught up, he was standing beside a young man in a white t-shirt and black sunglasses, leaning against a motorbike in a style reminiscent of the young Marlon Brando.

"Shambhala?" I asked, looking around for airport police, wondering if I was going to have to fight to get my bag back.

"Sure, man," he nodded.

"Well, where's the car?"

"No car, bike," he said, nodding to the motorbike on which he was leaning. "Hop on," he said, pointing to the vacant spot behind him.

I slung my backpack over my shoulder, and we lurched out of the airport. Buzzing down narrow streets, my long legs stuck out with knees barely missing goats and street vendors. I sent an affirmation skyward to my beloved mentor,

Saint Germain, please take command of this driver, and get me to the hotel safely!

Miraculously, in a few minutes we arrived at the Shambhala Hotel. It was not exactly the Shangri-La of *Lost Horizons*, but the room was clean.[6] I took a shower and then went out the back door to the flower garden. As I sipped a mango lassi, I noticed a heavy-set, middle-aged American woman sitting at a nearby table, who occasionally peered in my direction.

"You must be Peter?" she asked, introducing herself as Betty, and telling me that our guide, Steve, had told her to keep an eye out for a tall American. He would be there in the morning to take us to the airport. She said she was a Sunday school teacher from Bridgehampton, New York. As her husband didn't like to travel, every year she took a vacation by herself. Last year it was Club Med in the Caribbean. This year she wanted someplace more exotic. She seemed uncomfortable even in this semi-luxury hotel, and I wondered how she would fare in wilds of Tibet.

"What brought you here?" she asked.

I hesitated to say something too far out, but since we were going to travel together, I thought she might as well know right away who I was, so I blurted out, "A Tibetan lama appeared etherically and told me to visit his new incarnation here."

---

[6] *Lost Horizon*, by James Hilton, a novel written in 1933 about a paradise in a remote valley of Tibet. The author was supposedly partially inspired by a visit to the Mount Shasta area. Shambhala is a legendary utopian kingdom, rumored by the Tibetans to exist in the Himalayas or within the Earth. Trungpa Rinpoche talked about Shambhala as a state of being which, through our own consciousness, we create in everyday life.

Her look of panic suggested I should probably not mention either the command to seek a wish-fulfilling jewel or the appearance of the Dalai Lama. I'm sure she wondered if I was safe to travel with, but when I told her my baggage had been lost and I needed to get some clothes by morning, she offered to show me the shopping district down the street.

As we were starved and the sun was setting, we decided to eat first. In a small restaurant down a side street, the waitress handed us menus. Immediately, the lights went off and we were plunged into darkness. When the waitress came to take our order, I simply pointed blindly at the menu and prayed I would get something edible. A few candles were lit, but when our food arrived I still couldn't see what was on the plate. There were no utensils, so we ate with our fingers. I remembered a story I had heard of someone who had visited Nepal and almost died from a huge parasite.

Sitting in the dark with this Sunday school teacher that I seemed to have been sentenced to spend the next three weeks with, I took stock of the situation. Observing the in breath and out breath, the stream of anxious thoughts gradually slowed, and I felt a sense of peace. Out of the heart of my own basic goodness, I realized that the same goodness was also in Betty. We were both aspects of the same primordial consciousness, and I let go of my attachment to any particular outcome.

What are my choices? Actually, there are none.

If I leave the restaurant, where will I eat? Kathmandu is dark. I'm starving, and there is a warm meal in front of me. Everyone else seems to be enjoying themselves. I blocked out my mother's voice, warning not to eat in dirty places and the consequent fear of parasites. I let go of worries about the future and stopped trying to understand what was going on. In fact, I gave up trying to understand or make anything happen, and just rested in the fullness of the moment (a method called the Six Nails of Tilopa, described at the end of Chapter 11).

The meal turned out to be delicious, and just as we finished, the lights came on. We paid and left. As we headed back toward the hotel, we walked up a street lined with shops that were cubicles made of cloth hung from ropes. Everything was about to shut down, so I knew I had to hurry.

In one of these stalls I found most of the clothing I needed, except for a warm coat, so I signaled the Tibetan girl who had been sitting in the back of the shop. Just as I handed her my traveler's check and passport, the lights went out again and we were left in darkness. The girl disappeared. Would I ever see my money and passport again? My mind started imagining the worst. Without a passport, I couldn't get into Tibet. Had I come so far in my ancestor's footsteps, only to be turned back? Could I fly home without a passport? Once more, I realized there was no point worrying, as there was nothing I could do anyway. That act of surrender filled me with an inexplicable sense of joy.

Soon the girl reappeared, holding a kerosene lantern in one hand and the passport and change in the other. "I had to get change from my aunt down the street," she said, smiling sweetly, as she put the passport and change into my hand. As I parted the front flap to leave, she looked me in the eye and said, "I hope you find what you are looking for."

Did she know about the Wish-Fulfilling Jewel? I wanted to stay and talk to her, but Betty pulled on my sleeve, "Come on, we have to go; the hotel gate shuts soon."

As we walked up the road in the dark, I asked Betty if she had ever heard about something called the Wish-Fulfilling Jewel, but I immediately regretted speaking.

"Oh, some Buddhist superstition," she mumbled.

I should have known better than to mention something given on the inner planes to a stranger whose life revolved around the pursuit of worldly pleasures.

Next morning the lanky American guide, Steve, arrived. His shirt hung out over his baggy pants, and he wore a faded leather jacket, reminding me of Harrison Ford in the adventure film *Raiders of the Lost Ark*. He had that rugged appearance of a man who had seen a lot of life, yet who had achieved a sort of equanimity. I didn't know if this peaceful non-attachment was the result of years of travel or from his Buddhist practice. Planting his feet firmly on the floor, he put his hands on his hips and scanned the two of us. He apologized that since not enough people had signed up, the company was canceling the tour. Dejected, Betty said she was going to sue the company when she returned home.

"And why do you want to go to Tibet?" Steve asked, looking into my eyes.

"The Sixteenth Karmapa told me to go."

His face brightened, "The Sixteenth Karmapa was my guru," he said. "I was his English teacher. Since the lamas want me to teach the new Karmapa, I have to go see him anyway.[7] I can take you along, and we can visit some other places along the way."

"Sounds good to me," I said, feeling the Master's hand at work.

"What about you, Betty?" Steve asked.

"I suppose that would be alright," she agreed, not wanting to waste the money she had already spent on travel, and perhaps not wanting to admit failure to her husband, who had told her she was crazy to go to Tibet.

---

[7] The Karmapa lineage originated in the twelfth century and predates the lineage of Dalai Lamas by more than two hundred years. There is currently a legal dispute between rival factions of the Kagyu lineage, of which the Karmapa is traditionally the head, as to the identity of the authentic re-embodiment of the 17th Karmapa.

Chapter 2

Arrival in Lhasa

The next morning, we flew out of the Kathmandu airport and crossed the Himalayan range. Out the left window was Mount Everest, called by the Tibetans *Chomolungma,* Holy Mother. As the highest mountain in the world, she certainly deserved that name. Tibetans do not regard conquering mountain peaks to be a noble pastime, but as a sign of an inflated ego. Life is fragile enough without seeking additional challenges.

After four hours, the plane touched down at the Lhasa airport, which at 11,713 feet is one of the highest commercial airports in the world. We were met by the quiet, yet rugged looking Lobsang, who would be our driver; and Karma, the moon-faced young woman who would be our translator. Karma means action, or activity, not the good or bad consequences of action as interpreted in the West, and in Tibet it is a common girl's name. Steve dropped the hint that she hoped to find an American husband who would take her to America, but I felt no attraction to her, and when I shrugged, he let the subject drop.

Within an hour, we were passing beneath the arch that signaled the entrance of Lhasa. I wondered what ordeals my ancestor had endured to reach this arch in the eighteen hundreds, which I had attained so easily. While I was pondering what had driven him to make such a pilgrimage, we arrived at the hotel where we would spend our first night in the Tibetan capital. As we were going to leave in the morning, Karma volunteered to take me to the Barkhor open-air market surrounding the Jokhang Temple to help me find a *chuba* (warm coat).

Potala Palace, Lhasa

As we walked, she shared her view of marriage, "In Tibet, marriage is about survival, unless you are a monk and live in a monastery. Life is difficult here, and you can't survive alone. You need a partner, or even several partners. Many times when a woman marries, she also marries the man's brothers; or if there are many sisters they will share a husband. That way the children always have parents, even if one parent leaves or dies. Nowadays more people marry from love, but traditionally marriages are arranged."

"Wow, that wouldn't go over in the States," I said.

"Yes, it doesn't always work here either. Jealousy does not know borders. Sometimes people don't want to share. However, those who marry out of what you call 'chemistry' don't fare any better. Infatuation comes and goes. When it goes, who is going to take care of the children?

"Don't feel any pressure from me," Karma concluded, "I am only telling you this to give you a different view of life, and so you can think about what you truly want."

As I was letting her ideas sink in, we arrived at the Barkhor. Soon we found a rack of long silk chubas lined with white goat hair, and I found one that fit. Karma negotiated the price, and I walked away wearing the coat and feeling very Tibetan. This regal robe felt more uplifting than my lost parka. It emanated what the Tibetans call *lungta,* wind-horse, a horse that rides the wind, a non-physical quality that carries your aspirations upward. The prayer flags found all over Tibet are another manifestation of wind-horse. They believe that prayers and mantras written on the flags will be read and dispersed by the spirits of the air.

I was amazed that I hadn't seen any Chinese soldiers since arriving in Tibet, as I had read so much about their oppression of the people, and I had seen videos of their executions of lamas and destruction of temples. I mentioned this absence of the military to Karma.

"Oh, they're around," Karma said, with apprehension. "See those lamp poles? They contain video cameras that are monitored 24/7 by the police in that building at the side of the square. If you shout 'Free Tibet' or mention the Dalai Lama, soldiers will be here within fifteen seconds."

I had wanted to bring photos of the Dalai Lama with me to give out, as I had heard how the Tibetan people cherished him, but now Karma warned how dangerous that would have been. Anyone caught with his picture was beaten and imprisoned. Tourists caught with his picture were sometimes imprisoned and certainly expelled.

As we left the square, we passed tables filled with turquoise necklaces and exquisite silks. When I was surprised that many of the stalls were unattended, Karma said, "If someone steals, there is no trial, no plea bargaining; the Chinese just take the thief into the square and shoot him. Then they send the bill for the bullet to the thief's family. That type of justice really keeps down the crime rate."

"Yes, I'm sure it does," I said, agreeing with the obvious logic.

Barkhor, Behind Jokhang Temple

Chapter 3

Yambulagang

Our first stop was the Yambulagang Palace, which dominates the Yarlung Valley. It was the first large building in Tibet, built by King Nyatri Tsenpo around 127 BCE, and was the focus of the early *Bön* religion prior to the introduction of Buddhism.[8] It became the summer palace of King Songtsen Gampo and his two wives, one from Nepal, the other from China. These two women were the ones who first introduced Buddhism into Tibet. Later it was converted into the present monastery, which was destroyed by the Chinese along with six thousand other monasteries, but has since been rebuilt in its present form.

Short on breath, I struggled to climb the mountain that reached 11,000 feet above sea level, and as I climbed I kept thinking of the Wish-Fulfilling jewel I had been sent to Tibet to find. What would it look like? Would I have to dig it out of a mountain, or would it be handed to me by a yogi or high lama who was at this very moment most likely awaiting my arrival? Certainly, if I were going to find it anywhere, this magical building that had such a deep history could be the place.

After stopping many times to rest, I finally made it to the summit and flung open the door to the

---

[8] *Bön* was the tantric and shamanic tradition that existed in Northwestern Tibet prior to the introduction of the Indian teachings of tantra by Padmasambhava from the South. Some of the practices focus on working with nature spirits as well as the spirits of the dead.

monastery. It was not what I expected; no gilt statues of the Buddha or Padmasambhava resided on the altar and no elaborate *thangka*s graced the walls.[9] An old lama nodded as I glanced around, but he didn't seem to have been expecting me or show any sign of recognition. After a cursory tour of the empty room, I headed back down, feeling I had exhausted myself for nothing.

The view was so spectacular that I stopped at a switchback to sit for a while and contemplate. Was I really in Tibet? Was this a place my ancestor had visited a century before? I seemed to be in a dream; and as I tuned in to my breathing, I gradually fell into a natural meditation.

In breath, out breath—in breath, out breath—when a thought arose, I labeled it "thinking," and went back to observe my rhythmic breathing. I let go of all memories of the journey that had brought me here and of all thoughts about where I was going, and just followed the breath—no thoughts—no desire to understand, or to make anything happen. I just followed the breath, without any effort to alter it—letting awareness expand outward without limit.

Gradually the breath slowed, and my attention sank to the center of my chest, the focus of the Unfed Flame of the I AM Presence, and felt that awareness expanding outward—encompassing the mountain, the Yarlung valley, Tibet, China, India, the Earth, even the Universe.[10]

---

[9] *Thangka,* a tapestry, usually painted on silk or cotton, of a deity or mandala and used in meditation to invoke a particular consciousness.

[10] *Shamatha* (Sanskrit: calm, abiding peace), a preliminary practice of slowing the mind, usually by

Immersed in this joyous state, I was shocked to hear the voice of a girl say, "Mister, you like this?"

Standing in front of me was a girl about ten years old, with a large turquoise bead hanging from a thong around her sun-tanned neck. She held forward her open palm, which contained a magnificent crystal that filled her hand with pristine, radiant energy.

"I dug it here," she said proudly, pointing downward to the mountain.

Was this the Wish-Fulfilling Jewel?

I was about to pick it up, when suddenly Betty's plump hand closed over it. While meditating, I must have shut out the sound of her approach, and was now surprised to witness her dominating the moment. Holding the crystal away from my reach, she stuffed some Chinese money into the little girl's hand, who fled down the path to join her companions.

"I'm going to bring this home as a souvenir for my son," Betty said, placing the crystal into the zippered pouch of her fanny pack. "He loves crystals," she concluded, as though excusing her rudeness by her generosity to her son. "Come on," she urged, "Steve is waiting at the car."

I rose slowly, trying to make sense of what had just happened, and ambled slowly down the mountain, careful not to trip on the loose rock. Should I tell Betty that I thought the crystal was mine, that the child had offered it to me, not her? Then I remembered the teaching, *no one can deprive you of what is truly yours.*

---

observing the breath, and leading to *Vipassana* (Pali: insight), the realization of the nature of phenomena and the mind. Instruction can be obtained through Shambhala.org: shambhala.org/learn-to-meditate/

If that were true, then either that was not the Wish-Fulfilling jewel or the real one would come to me in some other way. I knew the Masters would not let me come all the way to Tibet to lose what they had sent me to obtain. I realized we had not yet seen the Karmapa at his monastery in Tsurphu, which would be a far more likely place to receive the jewel.

Yambulagang Palace, Yarlung Valley

Chapter 4

Crossing the Great Water

The next morning, we reached the Brahmaputra (Tibetan: *Tsangpo*), one of the four great rivers descending from the glaciers of Mount Kailash, long regarded by Tibetans and Indians as the center of the spiritual world. The river was wide, and during the time it took to cross, I fell into a natural stillness. I felt that in some way I was crossing a river within myself, leaving behind the limited self to enter a more expanded state of awareness, that I was *crossing the great water*, as symbolically described in the ancient Chinese book of wisdom, the *I Ching*. Around the middle of the river, the memory arose of the Wish-Fulfilling Jewel, and I asked Steve, "Is the Wish-Fulfilling Jewel real or simply a symbol?"

"Oh, it's very real," he said, "It's a medicine called the *Rinchen Ratna Samphel,* and it's supposedly made of 70 herbs, minerals, and purified metals—but I doubt it can fulfill wishes. In any case, in all my time in Tibet, I have never seen one. Few people know where the herbs grow or even how to make them. It's a very secret process, and the pills are very rare."

I sensed there was more to the Wish-Fulfilling Jewel than Steve realized. Why else would the Sixteenth Karmapa, supposedly a Buddha, appear and send me to Tibet to find one?

We soon arrived at Samye, the first Buddhist monastery in Tibet. King Trisong Detsen had begun construction in the year 767, but demons had repeatedly caused the foundation to crumble. He asked the monk Santaraksita, who practiced the *Sutrayana* form of Buddhism, which follows rules and precepts, to protect the construction, but to no avail. When Padmasambhava arrived, the near-mythical being who brought the Indian teachings of Tantra to Tibet, he performed the wrathful tantric ritual of Vajrakilaya, and subdued the demons. Chief among those demons was Pehar Gyalpo, whom he bound with an oath to protect the Dharma from henceforth. He also constructed *stupas* at each of the four cardinal directions, establishing a protective force field around the site.[11] Only by Padmasambhava's spiritual adeptship, which was far superior to Santaraksita's recitation of teachings, could the demons be subdued and the monastery completed.

The monks welcomed us, and one of them disappeared to fetch hot, salted yak butter tea. While we were waiting, we noticed above us on the shrine a statue of a naked male yogi with a naked female figure seated in his lap.

"That is called the *yab yum* pose (Tibetan: father-mother)," Steve said, "which is symbolic of the union of the male and female energies that you must learn to unite within yourself in order to attain enlightenment."

"Well, that's preferable to a naked man nailed to a cross that you see in Christian churches," I said.[12]

---

[11] Vajrakilaya is a meditational deity who wields a ritual dagger called a *phurba,* in order to cut through ignorance and liberate negative energies. He emits daggers of blue light. The energy is similar to that of the western Archangel Michael, who wields the Sword of Blue Flame.

[12] The vertical and horizontal beams of the cross also represent the male and female aspects. Prior to Christianity,

"Yes, Tantric Buddhism is not based on denial, but the acceptance of all aspects of life. It teaches the transmutation of sexual into spiritual energy," Steve continued. "In fact, sexual energy is just the life force manifesting through the second chakra. On the path to enlightenment, a yogi learns to circulate that energy through the microcosmic orbit: down from the solar plexus to the root chakra, then up the central channel in the back, to the pineal gland, and down the front—returning the energy to the solar plexus. That is why you to put the tip of your tongue against the roof of your mouth when you meditate, to complete this circuit."[13]

---

the beams were of equal length, but under the Christian patriarchy the horizontal, feminine beam, was shortened. Originally, no human form was on the cross, although occasionally a sacrificial lamb. Depictions of a human figure did not appear on the cross for about two hundred years after the supposed crucifixion.

[13] *Tantra* (Sanskrit: web, weave) is a practice that originated in India and Afghanistan, and which became known in Tibet as *Vajrayana* (Sanskrit: indestructible vehicle, the Way of the Lightning Bolt). Tantra weaves together in ritual meditation the use of *mantra* (sacred word or sound), *mudra* (gesture), and *yantra* (mystical visualizations, diagrams, and mandalas) in order to reveal the true nature of mind. Unlike the *Hinayana* (lesser vehicle), where enlightenment is pursued solely for one's own liberation, in Vajrayana as well as Mahayana (greater vehicle) one's efforts are dedicated for the benefit of others. Tantric practice is in contrast to the worship of an external deity, for the practitioner strives to see Divinity in everything, the outer and inner realities seen as one.

"A yogi does not need to unite with another physical body. He or she first visualizes the luminous light body, and then visualizes union with the Deity that is the feminine or masculine counterpart. Meditating together, they circulate energy through their unified channels. Through this practice, you attain a luminous body that emits rainbow rays to bless creation.

Yam Yum Meditation on inner union

While the others waited, I felt pulled to explore a nearby alcove. It was dimly lit by a few butter lamps, and as I backed up to leave, I bumped into something solid. Whirling around, there overhead was the night-black demon with the crown of skulls that had appeared in my bedroom to prevent me from coming to Tibet. I had disobeyed him, and now here he was, glowered down with bared fangs, with his sword poised to descend.

Had one of the demons subdued by Padmasambhava escaped after all? I whirled around and fled back into the shrine room. Looking back to see if the being was following, I realized that the fearsome being had been a statue of Mahakala (Sanskrit: *Maha*, great; *Kala*, time, darkness), a Deity whose original purpose was to remind one of the illusory nature of human existence. The five skulls represented the five afflictive emotions that must be transmuted into the five wisdoms (ignorance into wisdom, pride into equanimity, anger into patience, attachment into patience, envy into joy).

I was glad to rejoin the others, who sat chatting with a monk before five cups of tea. I picked up the one closest, and as I sipped the hot liquid began to feel my self-confidence return. Steve was explaining that prior to Buddhism, the shamanic practices of Bön were employed to create powerful entities that would do the bidding of the shaman. Sometimes they would even wage war against each other, or attack competing shamans. These demons were humanly created thought forms that could take on a life of their own. They could be protectors as well as terrifying opponents, depending on the consciousness with which they were created, and if the entity perceived one as friend or foe. The first things Padmasambhava did when he entered Tibet was subdue these demons and compel them to protect the Dharma. Subsequent generations of Buddhist practitioners began to invoke these beings, called *Dharmapalas,* for protection. However, depending on the unresolved neuroses of the individual practitioner, these thought-forms can take on completely different attributes. In a sense, they live on the thoughts and emotions of their devotees. Although they were invoked to destroy anyone who tried to distort the spiritual teachings, who is to say what else they are capable of?[14]

Eventually, these shamanic practices became tantric rituals, which utilized the images of the demons as aspects of consciousness, projections of one's own emotions. As everyone must confront and dissolve their demons sooner or later, seeing their image as big as life before one facilitates that process of liberation. Avoiding that confrontation perpetuates lifelong possession by these unconscious drives, appearing as emotional habits that poison all relationships.

Steve continued to talk about Padmasambhava's prophecy about a future invasion of Tibet. In trying to avert that invasion, the shamans had done *pujas* (rituals) to invoke Mahakala to keep out foreigners. The famous prophecy, given almost 1,200 years prior to fulfillment by the Communist invasion in 1950, warned that:

The Land of Snows (Tibet) will be overrun by foreigners. In that distant day when horses run on wheels and the iron bird flies, the

---

[14] These protector demons eventually achieved liberation, according to Tai Situ Rinpoche in a discussion I had with him at Karma Triyana Dharmachakra in Woodstock, NY.

Tibetan people will be scattered like ants across the face of the earth, and the dharma will move to the land of the red man.

Wanting to avert that invasion, every effort was made to keep foreigners away. Of course, little mention is made that during the T'ang dynasty (618-906), Tibetan warriors invaded China. During the Qing Dynasty, China actually supported the Dalai Lama and kept him in power. Russia and Britain also invaded Tibet. Even though the invasion by the Communists caused great suffering, the destruction of monasteries, and loss of life, it also forced many lamas to leave Tibet and finally share their wisdom with the world.

Seeing that I had finished my tea, the monk refilled my cup. I was puzzled that none of the others tasted their tea. According to the way I had been raised, to not even taste what one was offered was an insult. As we left, I asked Betty why she had neglected her tea.

"When it was poured, it was full of flies that floated on top. The monk skimmed them out with his hand. After that none of us felt like drinking."

After my confrontation with the six-armed being who appeared as Mahakala, the purity of the tea was of no concern. I could die at any moment, but probably not from drinking a cup of tea.

At a monastery in Central Tibet

Chapter 5

Saved by a Yidam

The original plan was to go to Shigatse, a two-day drive west of Lhasa, but since the planned tour had been cancelled, we were free to go wherever spirit led. I had been looking forward to visiting Shigatse, where master Kuthumi Lal Singh had resided prior to ascending. He had an organ in his home on the edge of town, which he played when communicating telepathically with his students around the world. They would hear the inward music, and then go into meditation to attune to his mind. A few of those close to Madame Blavatsky (founder of the Theosophical Society) had attempted to trek into Tibet to visit him, but had been turned back by severe storms, bandits, and demons.

Steve said that any house of Kuthumi's would long since have been replaced by housing for the Chinese. Even though gone from the physical plane, one never knows when a being who is master over space, time, and energy will appear in whatever form they choose. In fact, during my early apprenticeship, I had met Kuthumi in physical form on at least two previous occasions. To visit his former home would, I thought, make a physical encounter more likely; however, I had learned over time that Masters never appear to satisfy human desire, but only for some higher purpose.

Now, however, Steve wanted to skip Shigatse, which he said had become a large commercial town largely populated by Chinese settlers. Instead, he wanted to venture over the mountains to Lake Namtso, a spiritual focus where supernatural beings were said to reside. In that rarified atmosphere, accomplished tantric practitioners could even see their thoughts, he said. In tantric *Vajrayana* practice, you generate a Deity, called a *yidam,* from your mind. Once established in consciousness, you then merge with it and receive its unique attributes. A skillful yogi can generate such a visualization so clearly that it can even be seen by others.

Since he didn't want to dominate our plans, even though he was our guide, Steve insisted we vote on where to go. As Betty and I were the only two voting, the agreement had to be unanimous. Betty shrugged and said that she didn't care. No doubt she wished she had returned to the Caribbean this year instead of choosing to go to Tibet, but destiny had other plans for her.[15]

We finished breakfast and loaded up the car to set out for Lake Namtso. Even though it was late August, the morning air was frigid and I wrapped my new chuba about me. Steve suggested I take the front seat because of my long legs, so I sat next to Lobsang. I saw the tires were bald as I got in, and I hoped that the pass we had to cross would be clear of snow.

Lake Namtso was only 144 miles northwest of Lhasa, but when traveling over dirt roads, distances can be deceptive. It was not until afternoon that we reached the cutoff from the dirt highway to ascend the 15,000-foot Largen-La Pass. We had to surmount that obstacle

---

[15] Free will is achieved in how we process the events of our lives, if we grow from them or not. The main circumstances of our lives: parents, partners, occupations, etc., are prearranged prior to birth according to the karmic lessons we have chosen to learn.

before we could descend the other side of the mountain range to Lake Namtso.

The sky darkened as we drove. Black clouds were gathering over the mountains ahead. I pulled the sash of my robe tighter and prayed to the being known as Mighty Hercules to get us over the mountains. Godfre Ray King had spoken of Hercules as a Deity who could appear to give direct assistance, especially where superhuman strength was required. I visualized him as the hero from Greek mythology who had been assigned twelve humanly impossible labors, one of which was to subdue a wild bull on the island of Crete. Could I invoke him the way the Tibetans invoked yidams? I decided to try.

Ascending the icy road into the mountains, the car began to slip from side to side. I tuned in to my I AM Presence, whose flame I could feel in the center of my chest, and continued to visualize the Greek hero who had subdued the mythical bull, and to call on him to manifest.

From the ominous clouds, a light snow began falling. Betty glowered from the back seat, as if saying, "I told you we should have stayed with the original plan and gone to Shigatse."

With wheels spinning furiously and the car lurching from one side of the road to the other, we reached the summit, and Steve shouted to Lobsang to pull over. To stop before the car crossed the summit and faced down the other side was a mistake, I felt, but we coasted to a stop on a plateau covered with packed snow. I stepped out of the car and found we were inside a cloud, white in every direction. At an altitude over 15,000 feet, the air was thin, and I took slow, deliberate breaths. The snow now began to fall in earnest.

There was nothing to see, so we piled back in the car. Lobsang started the engine, but when he pressed the accelerator the wheels spun and the car remained in place. We got out and pushed, but could not get any traction. As Steve and Lobsang discussed the situation, I walked to the top of the ridge to ask for guidance. As I turned my attention inward, I realized the seriousness of our situation. We hadn't seen any other cars since turning off the main road. It was late, and night was approaching. People froze on these passes, their bodies found when the snow melted in spring. Was this where my life was to end? I had heard that when you freeze to death it is painless, that you simply fall sleep. I began looking for a good place to lie down, but everything was barren and windswept.

I breathed slowly, savoring each breath, feeling the preciousness of life. Only a moment ago, I was a kid, it seemed, trying to figure out what to do with my life. I felt that only now was I beginning to figure out why I was here. I called to Saint Germain, "Is this where my work with you is to end?"

A blast of thunder ended that reverie, as if he were reminding me to call on my Higher Self. Once more I turned my attention inward and invoked Hercules. Shouting to the heavens, I cried out,

Mighty Hercules, come forth!
I AM the Presence of Hercules in action!

Immediately my ears were greeted by the welcome hum of an approaching high-powered vehicle. Soon a black Ford Bronco sped up the road, obviously equipped with snow tires and four-wheel drive. It pulled to a stop, and out of each of the four doors emerged a muscular Chinese man, each wearing an identical black leather jacket and a Chicago Bulls baseball cap. The driver stomped up the hill and stopped in front of me. I found myself staring at the snorting face of the red bull on his cap.

He gave me a piercing look, and inwardly I heard him ask, "You called?"

He gave a small laugh, then turned around and descended to his car. The other three men who appeared and seemed identical to him piled in and the engine roared to life. The Bronco made a U-turn so the front bumper was against the front bumper of our car. Lobsang started the engine and put the gears in neutral, and they pushed our car back around so it faced down the way we had come. Our rescuer's car disengaged and, with a farewell toot of the horn, started back downhill, soon disappearing into the emptiness. In frozen silence, we followed, no one saying a word. When we reached the valley and rejoined the main road, Steve asked, "Anyone hungry?"

We had not eaten since leaving Lhasa that morning, and gladly accepted his suggestion to eat in the town ahead. It was one of the new Chinese towns that, until recently, had been only a gathering place of wandering *drokpas* (Tibetan: people of the solitudes, nomads). We went to the only restaurant in town, and it was packed. Soon, however, we were brought plates of steaming noodles. They were bland, without any seasoning, so after the first bite, I decided to try the sauce that was in a small dish on the table. As I heaped a spoonful on the side of my plate, Steve said, "Careful of that."

Chilled to the bone, I welcomed the idea of something warming, so I dipped a chopstick in the brown paste and dabbed a drop on my tongue. At that moment I felt that a hot nail had been driven through the top of my skull and down into my brain. A white light appeared above my head and I jumped up. I knocked the chair back and ran out of the restaurant into the street and cold night air.

Gradually the incendiary effect of the chili dissipated, and the light faded to a glow within the center of my skull. I laughed at the thought of attaining enlightenment, not from the mythical Wish-Fulfilling Jewel, or from the touch of the Karmapa, but from the hot chili sauce in a Chinese restaurant.

Then it struck me how the Ford Bronco had appeared to save us at the moment I had visualized and invoked Hercules, and I remembered the red face of the bull on the hats of the Chinese men. The yidam seemed to have manifested according to the prescribed method. Or, had that actually been Saint Germain? According to tantric theory, Saint Germain, the yidam, and my own I AM Presence were all one consciousness that could manifest individually or separately. Whoever it was that had appeared, I thanked the Master Saint Germain, the yidam Hercules, and my own unlimited self for assistance.

The light in my head had finally dimmed, and I realized that I was standing in the gutter of the street. The snow squall had passed, and I could now see the stars overhead. Beneath their display, I felt like an insignificant speck. Inhaling a few breaths of the thin air, I went back inside to rejoin my companions and finish dinner.

48

Chapter 6

At the Feet of the Karmapa

Steve had written ahead to the monastery at Tsurphu and arranged for us to have a private audience with the fifteen-year-old Seventeenth Karmapa, supposedly the reincarnation of the previous Karmapa who had appeared to me in meditation. Since he was the one who had initiated this journey, I was sure that something profound would happen. He would give me some profound message or transmission of enlightenment. If he did not give me a Precious Wish-Fulfilling Jewel, at the very least he would tell me where to find one.

We spent that night at what the tour company described in their brochure as a "quaint mountain inn where the guide will prepare a mouth-watering dinner of local Tibetan delicacies." The inn turned out to be a rickety structure lashed together with rope, and dinner was a can of fruit cup and a couple of dry biscuits. We had to climb a ladder to reach a scaffold to get to our bedrooms. Flopping on the thin mattress, I looked up through holes in the straw roof at the glimmering stars.

In the middle of the night, I awakened in a panic to find that my lungs had stopped. With breathing paralyzed, I knew that in a few seconds I would pass out. Desperate, I pounded both fists into my chest as hard as I could. With the second blow, breathing began and I sat up, gasping for air. Terrified to go back to sleep, I focused on breathing. Many westerners had similar problems with altitude sickness. I had just heard of a woman who went to bed on her first night in Lhasa, and when her husband shook her in the morning, she was dead. I sat up for the remainder of the night, wondering if I was going to make it through the trip.

In the morning, after another meal of biscuits and fruit cup, we set out on the long drive to Tsurphu. There was a hole in the car's exhaust pipe, so the interior filled with fumes. Lobsang frequently lowered the window until we complained of the cold, and then he would close the window until we again complained of the fumes. We arrived finally at the winding road leading up the valley to Tsurphu. As we pulled up in front of the monastery, the monks greeted Steve, who was well known here. We had to wait for the morning rituals to complete, and then would be allowed to enter. I paced nervously around the courtyard, wondering why this living Buddha had called me here, and what he would reveal. Surely, he already was aware I was waiting outside.

A couple of the young monks played Frisbee, surely inappropriate outside the temple of a Buddha. Yet, when one of the monks threw the orange disc, I caught it and threw it back. I was sure a senior lama would soon emerge and stop the sport, but in the meantime, they continued to run around and joke as though this was some ordinary place.

Soon bells rang and the great doors opened. High lamas escorted our small group into the temple. On the elevated, gilt throne, sat the Karmapa. I had expected a radiant being, but he seemed more like an ordinary kid being forced to meet guests, when he would obviously have preferred being outside playing Frisbee with the other monks. We made the customary prostrations, then went forward one at a time, and the kid thumped us on the head one at a time with his metal *dorje*.[16] To my disappointment, there was no sudden realization. Soon this outer ceremony was over, and we were led into an inner chamber for our interview.

Still wearing his magnificent gilded robe, the Karmapa sat on a chair before us, lamas on either side. When he asked if we had any questions, Steve spoke. He was obviously held in high regard for his years of service to the previous Karmapa, and now asked when he was to begin giving the requested English lessons. When they told him that the lessons would have to be delayed, they didn't explain that was because they were planning his escape from Tibet.[17]

Then I was asked, "Do you have any questions?"

Reluctant to say anything, as I was sure he already knew everything about me, including my present thoughts, I waited for him to speak. I waited for his message, but after a painful silence, I blurted out "Your Holiness, I have come as you requested."

"What?" he asked, a look of surprise on his face.

"Remember, you asked me to come here?"

---

[16] *Dorje* (Tibetan: indestructible, diamond-like; Sanskrit: *Vajra*). A ritual object made of metal with prongs at either end, one end symbolizing the phenomenal world of *samsara*, the other end the noumenal world of *nirvana*, enlightened awareness. In the middle is a jewel representing *sunyata*, the emptiness from which everything originates. In Indian mythology the vajra was a weapon, but now is used symbolically to represent the destruction of illusion through sudden enlightenment.

[17] The escape of the Karmapa (Ogyen Trinley Dorje) had to be postponed until the night of December 30th, 1999.

He looked to both lamas for guidance, but they shrugged. Looking back, he said, "I don't know what you're talking about."

Had this journey to Tibet been some sort of cosmic joke, I wondered, as he looked at me with a blank stare? There was nothing more to say, and it seemed the interview was over. The elder monks left the room and the Karmapa rose to leave also. Desperate, I breached the protocol and walked directly up to him and said, "So, if you didn't call me, why am I here?"

"How should I know?" he shrugged, and turned his back and walked out the door.

I was stunned. Steve and the others had gone outside, and I now followed. The young monks were still playing Frisbee, and as one prepared to throw the disc in my direction, I shook my head. I could not think of playing at such a moment. What was I doing here? I had been guided to come to Tibet to see this being, but why? Perhaps if I found the Wish-Fulfilling Jewel, all would be revealed.

We returned to the car and drove downhill to the main road that meandered into the wide-open Tibetan plains. Silently I prayed,

*Saint Germain, please take complete command
of this situation, and reveal the purpose
for which I have been brought here.*

*I AM God directed and God commanded.
I AM the Great Divine Director
of my life, activity, and world.*

The dirt road seemed never-ending. We had run out of food, as both Steve and Karma each thought the other had put the second box in the car, but it had been left in front of the hotel back in Lhasa. By the next day my stomach was an empty cavern and my arms and legs were becoming numb with cold. I affirmed, *I am the Presence of God bringing me something to eat.*

Suddenly I felt the unmistakable presence of Sathya Sai Baba. His presence was as clear as when I sat before him at his ashram in Puttaparthi, India, years before. When I left, he had said, "Have no fear, I am with you." Now, he was true to his word.

"Baba, I'm hungry," I said silently.

"Open the glove compartment," he said.

"But, it's not my car; I can't do that, " I protested.

"I said, open the glove compartment."

"Okay," I said, heeding his instruction, and pushed on the release button. The door flopped open, revealing a package of milk biscuits.

"That's hardly going to fill my stomach," I thought.

"Eat one," he said.

I opened the package and drew out one of the thin cookies, and found stamped across the face of the biscuit the word, "BABA." Looking at the wrapper, I saw they were called Baba Biscuits. The cookie dissolved in my mouth, having the effect of a sacrament. I felt a wave of Sai Baba's grace, and with it came the realization that the nomads we occasionally passed looked well fed, and that they must have food they would share.

We rounded a bend and I saw a group of these nomads. A few were tending yaks near a group of yurts, and I shouted, "Stop the car!"

Lobsang did not need a translation, and pulled over.

"Steve, they must have food. Let's ask them for something to eat."

Everyone except Betty got out, and she remained scowling in the back seat, munching on the newly found cookies. People began emerging from the yurts to see what we wanted.

Steve went up to a man standing in front of a yurt and talked with him. Then he beckoned. The man threw an animal skin onto a shallow pile of dried yak dung, indicating it was a soft place where we should sit. As smoothly as if we had arrived at a restaurant, a beautiful Tibetan girl emerged from the yurt with a pot of steaming hot yak butter tea, and poured us each a bowl. Lobsang had gone back to the car and now returned. To my great surprise, he was holding a cloth sack of *tsampa,* the roasted Barley flour that is the staple food of the Tibetan people. He always disappeared when we ate, and I had not seen him eat during the entire trip. He must have gone off by himself to eat this tsampa that had been stashed under his seat. The kind man kneeled down and demonstrated how to mix the flour in the salted yak butter tea. You formed a ball, which you then popped in your mouth. It was delicious, reminding me of the Pablum cereal that my mother used to spoon-feed me as a two-year-old. Later, I had been unable to find it in any store. Now that nourishment served to me by my mother was being served again by nomads in Tibet.

Warmth began returning to my body, and I looked up at the girl who had served the tea. She was watching attentively to see if there was anything else we needed, and her attentiveness reminded me again of the nurturing I had received from my mother. She wore the traditional black dress, covered by a colorful apron. A necklace of turquoise nuggets graced her neck. An extraordinary beauty radiated from her clear eyes. Unlike many beautiful women in the West, whose flirtatiousness is a part of their personality, she seemed to not be aware of her beauty. In this rugged environment, where survival depends largely on skill, strength, trust and compassion, an ephemeral quality such as beauty is not highly prized. The Buddhist culture regards attachment to such temporary qualities as one of the causes of dissatisfaction and unhappiness.

Suddenly attracted to this woman who was such an unusual combination of strength and gentleness, I wondered what life would be like with her.

I asked Steve how old he thought she was, and if she was single.

"Why, do you like her?"

"Well, she is certainly very fine."

For Steve, who had been thinking of taking monks vows when he returned to Tsurphu, the woman held no interest for him. However, without a moment's hesitation, he shouted to the man who had welcomed us, probably the girl's father, "Hey, is your daughter single?"

The man nodded, pushing the girl forward. Understanding immediately that she was being offered, she stood silently looking at the ground, a blush on her cheeks. The other nomads who had been watching us eat also realized that the life of this girl, who was a part of their community, might suddenly change. These mountain people were used to abrupt changes. Accidents, deaths, as well as opportunities such as this could arise without notice; and they knew that when an opportunity arose it had to be grasped before it disappeared. It could be the opportunity to sell a prize yak or make a favorable marriage for your daughter.

Gradually a new vision of my life began unfolding in my mind's eye, one in which I was no longer on a spiritual quest, but where I had a job to earn enough to support a wife and children. I could no longer travel to the places I had visited in the past, such as India, Egypt, and Lake Titicaca. There was no more meditating in my shrine room, which was now converted into a children's bedroom. The guest room was now home to her family, whom I had imported. Of course, it is the duty of the husband to assist the girl's parents and grandparents, and take care of them as they age.

The vision dissolved as I awakened from the daydream. Sensing the opportunity had passed, the girl stepped back to rejoin her father. Steve and I rose and thanked these kind people for their hospitality, and returned to the car. We still had another hour's drive before reaching Tidrum. This was the mountain retreat where Padmasambhava and his consort Yeshe Tsogyal meditated and gave teachings to each other.

We finally arrived at Tidrum, where we had been invited to stay at the nunnery. A couple of the robust nuns met us in the parking area. They hefted our luggage onto their backs and marched uphill to the convent. When I tried to carry my own bag, the nun laughed and kept on walking. These were mountain girls, and well adapted to the altitude. I was breathing deeply carrying nothing but my body up hill. When we arrived at the convent, a few nuns vacated a room for us.

Dakini Khandro Tsering Chodron.

Below the *gonpa* (temple) was a glacier fed stream that raged down the mountain valley. On the far bank, I found the hot mineral spring where they said Padmasambhava used to soak. A small pool had been hollowed out of the riverbank, and in the center of it was the rock on which he sat. I waded into the warm water and was soon sitting on his seat. This inspired me to invoke his presence—to call forth the great mahasiddha who brought Vajrayana Buddhism to Tibet. No sooner did I have that thought than the etheric form of Padmasambhava appeared. His form suddenly merged with my own form, and I was Padmasambhava, sitting on the rock, as in ages past. I began chanting the Vajra Guru Mantra, that he had said was the fastest path to liberation:

Om Ah Hung Vajra Guru
Padma Siddhi Hung.

(Om Ahh Hoong Vaaj-ra Guru Paadma Siddhi Hoong).

The vibrations of the Sanskrit manifested the awareness of the three worlds of body, speech, and mind: *Om,* invoking transcendental consciousness; *Ah,* invoking Divine will in the vocal center in the throat; and *Hung,* awakening compassion in the heart; *Vajra Guru* the lightning-like awareness of the universal teacher that can liberate instantaneously; *Padma* the lotus of the Divine Mother which is the source of manifestation, the ground of wisdom, and the means to the power of accomplishment signified by *Siddhi.* With the final *Hung,* the omniscient guru manifests as the self. [18] After a while Padmasambhava's energy dissipated, and the form sitting on the rock appeared once again as myself. However, I felt altered, sensing I was in the center of a mandala in which all would unfold perfectly.[19]

The sun was now going down, so I dressed and climbed back up the hill, feeling profoundly altered. The nuns had graciously prepared *momos* for dinner, a kind of dumpling, which I ate with great relish.

That night the Master Saint Germain appeared in a dream and revealed a past life in which we had both been monks together in Tibet. We had taken the Bodhisattva vow to achieve enlightenment so that we could work for the benefit of others, not only in that life, but in future lives as well. Little had we known that in a far distant time he would appear to me in a redwood forest in California and reawaken me to that vow. He offered liberation, but once he revealed the suffering of the world, I agreed to remain and receive

---

[18] The true meaning of a mantra cannot be translated, as it is a vibration that invokes a state of awareness. The Vajra Guru Mantra has many different interpretations and levels of meaning; however, knowledge of these meanings is not necessary in order to benefit. The vibration of the syllables is the direct manifestation of the mind of the omnipresent guru.

[19] *Mandala* (Sanskrit: circle), a circular pattern, often represented artistically, which is visualized to create a circle of consciousness and energy representative of one's relationship to a specific aspect of reality.

training so that I could be of greater service to him in his work for humanity.[20]

He explained that this trip to Tibet was not the fiasco it seemed, but part of that training. He said he had given Guy Ballard (aka Godfre Ray King) some of the core Vajrayana teachings in the 1930s, but had been limited by the materialism of the times from giving more than the basics. Now, he wished me to reveal further teachings, many of which had been preserved in Tibet for the past twelve hundred years. He wanted these teachings on the nature of mind and the mastery of illusory phenomena to be given clearly, free of the cultural associations of Asia, and in a manner westerners could easily understand. In bringing me to the location where I had received these teachings in a past life, he said that their essence, which was still latent in my mind, would arise spontaneously.

Saint Germain concluded by saying, "My boy, I know you often feel alone, but know I am assisting you to the extent I am able without interfering with the challenges that are required for your acquisition of wisdom."

Just before morning, I had another dream in which I saw the face of a tall *naljorpa* (yogi) with dreadlocks coiled on top of his head. His eyes penetrated mine, and he said, "I'll be waiting."

---

[20] This meeting where Saint Germain materialized before me in a physical body is recounted in my book *Apprentice to the Masters: Adventures of a Western Mystic, Book ll*. This book also gives further teachings of the Ascended Masters that were transmitted through direct inner and outer contact.

Chapter 7

Encountering a Naljorpa

The next morning I rose early, and as it was cold, wrapped myself in my chuba. I felt a pull to walk up the path on the far side of the river that led further into the mountains. It was what some call a gut feeling, although it came from the center of my chest. I had learned that even though I knew how to contact the Masters, guidance in most everyday situations comes through following this inner feeling. After a half hour climb, I stopped to catch my breath and watch the sun rise over the Himalayan peaks. I soon had the feeling that I was being watched. Looking around, I saw there was a cave up the slope. In its entrance, a man with dreadlocks stared at me. This must be the naljorpa I had seen in my dream, one of those rare beings that inhabit remote parts of Tibet. Surely, this must be where the Presence had been guiding me.

I had heard that these yogis practice the Six Yogas of Naropa, the generation of inner heat (*Tummo*) being only the first practice toward full mastery of body and mind.[21] Steve had said that when Naropa began his spiritual quest he underwent twelve ordeals, each of which taught an essential lesson. After meeting his guru, Tilopa, he underwent an additional twelve major ordeals, which eventually prepared him for mastery.

Fascinated by the powerful, yet serene energy of this yogi, I scrambled up the loose rock until I stood

---

[21] Naropa (1016-circa1100 CE), disciple of Tilopa, spiritual consort of Niguma. Subsequent students of his teachings were Marpa, and his student, Milarepa.

before him. He sat in lotus posture on a flat boulder, wearing only a loincloth and a thin shawl around his shoulders. He continued to gaze as I approached, and then beckoned for me to sit beside him. I sat on the edge of his boulder with my feet on the icy ground.

Soon I was enveloped in a blanket of warmth. The yogi said nothing, but I felt so warm I took off my chuba. This was the technique of tummo I had heard about that was known as the first yoga of Naropa, and I wondered if he would teach it to me. It would certainly be useful in dealing with the cold winters back home. No sooner had this thought passed through my mind than he said, "Yes, I could teach you, but you would have to practice for three years on retreat without heat or hot water. You can stay here in my cave. There's plenty of room. Are you ready?"

As I toyed with the idea, he said, "People say they want to go on retreat, but when I offer them a place, they say they will think about it, but none come back. Go ahead, have a look around. Maybe you'll want to stay," he laughed.

I rose and entered the cave. On one side was a mat covered with a cotton shawl, and a rock served as a shrine on which was a picture of Padmasambhava and his consort, Yeshe Tsogyal. Beside it were a bell, dorje, and some loose-leaf texts. There were no cooking implements, and I wondered if he was one of those yogis who absorb his nourishment directly from the Source.

I sat down in the back of the cave, imagining what it would be like to be on retreat here, probably surviving only on tsampa. I drew my chuba around me, as it had become cold as soon as I had left his presence, and I turned my attention inward. With no distractions, meditation came easily, and I was soon free of thought. Effortlessly, I soon found myself free of body awareness, free of self—simply as awareness observing waves of light flowing through boundless reaches of space—all was permeated by the all-pervasive drone of the cosmic OM, as from some omnipresent tambura. There was only being—and consciousness, wisdom, and bliss.

For how long this immersion in pure being lasted I do not know, but after a while I became aware as an observer again, of self and other. There were other non-physical intelligences with whom I was in mental contact, and looking down, I saw the blue ball of earth below. This is what I had experienced prior to taking birth in this lifetime. As I became more focused, I began to feel that familiar brotherly feeling of the Master Saint Germain, and looking up, saw his etheric white-robed form. Beside him was the Master Jesus, and on the other side a feminine being I recognized as Nada.

They smiled, and I nodded back. I felt only love—with no compulsion to bow, as religions teach. They were not promoting any religious worship, but were motivated solely by the desire to liberate humanity from ignorance, and awaken people to their own true Master potential.

Gradually these noble beings faded, and I became aware again of a body—a pain in my ankle from a pebble on which it had been lying. I moved it and stretched my legs, coming back fully into the relative world. I reflected on how in that consciousness of the One, there had been no compulsion to recite affirmations or to try to make something happen. In that state of being, any thought would have manifested immediately, but there was no thought.

I emerged from the cave just as the sun rose above the ridge of the mountains, and the naljorpa asked, "Ready for retreat?"

I shook my head, knowing that my work was still in the world. I thanked him with one of the few Tibetan phrases I knew, *"Tashi delek,"* meaning, "May auspiciousness be yours."

A blast of cold wind blew around the peak and down my neck, and I tightened the rope that held the folds of my chuba together, and began my descent. I had wondered for many years if there were still such legendary beings as this naljorpa alive somewhere in the mountains, and now I knew.

Chapter 8

Mahakala Returns

The nuns had brought hot tea and tsampa to our room, which I mixed together to make a delicious meal. After we had eaten, we joined the nuns in their shrine room, where they were beginning their daily practice. Betty sat with Karma and the nuns on one side, while Steve, Lobsang, and I sat on the other. From the altar, clouds of smoke rose from the incense, carrying our prayers to the Gods. Trumpets sounded sporadically as the drums banged out a rhythm in the manner that short-circuits the mind's attempt at thought. Becoming absorbed in the stillness, my breath began to slow.

Suddenly, once again, the terrifying form of Mahakala was leering down on me.

"In the name of the living Christ, I command you to leave," I shouted, but he threw back his head and laughed.

"Dear God, please help," I cried out.

"There is no God outside your own mind," he jeered.

His eyes grew bright with inner fire as he raised his sword, perhaps to add my head to the collection of skulls he wore around his neck.

A voice on my right said, "Turn your attention inward."

Beside me, I recognized the naljorpa from my visit to the cave that morning. He repeated, "Turn your attention inward to the center of your being, and see what arises."

I remembered the fear of the dark outside the back door when, as a child, my mother asked me to take the trash out after dinner. I would go out into the dark and walk down the steps. The lid of the garbage can always stuck. While I was trying to pry it off, something always moved in the bushes. Was it a branch blowing in the breeze, or was it an evil demon? I wrenched off the lid, dropped in the garbage, then ran back up the steps into the light of the kitchen. Breathless, I slammed the door and pretended that nothing had happened.

I also remembered lying in bed and feeling something in the room. As it moved closer, I pulled the sheet over my head, hoping whatever it was would go away. Then, I remembered a past life in which I had been a powerful shaman who had created a demon to terrorize those who had harmed my family. In fact, it resembled this very demon.

"Feel your heart," the naljorpa whispered, "only your love will protect you."

I looked up into the face of the living Mahakala, and realized that I had created the energy of this yidam ages ago, that now appeared as Mahakala. I had projected my fear onto this image. It took different forms through many lifetimes. It was the one that used to wait for me by the garbage cans that haunted my bedroom at night, and used to drain my energy when I watched a scary movie. It was my creation that I maintained by fear. I was filled with sadness over this neglected part of myself.

"All my many lives, you have been following me. Now we finally meet, and I see that I am your creator. By the power of God That I AM, I now dissolve you."

Shocked, the demon stumbled backward a step.

Focusing my attention on love, I felt a golden sun in the center of my chest. From that sun I sent a shaft of light to this part of myself appearing as Mahakala, piercing its heart. Through the use of visualization, I enveloped him in a luminous, golden aura, surrounded by pink light. His face changed; it was no longer terrifying, but peaceful. As I continued to send this tangible love substance, he stepped back. A wave of compassion went out to him, and I said, "I love you."

For a brief moment he looked almost human, then clasped his hands in prayer, bowed, and was gone.

There was a pain in my chest. As I looked around, I found that I was lying on the floor, several nuns looking down. Steve was sitting beside me, pressing on my sternum. As I had sunk into meditation and my breathing slowed, I had passed out. I took in deep breaths, struggling to revive. The tough, head nun shook a thick, weathered finger, "No more meditation for you."

I looked around for the naljorpa, but he was gone. He must have been present in his light body. Or, perhaps he had only been in my mind—the same place as the demon.

Chapter 9

The Essence of Tantra

In an attempt to fully return to body consciousness, I walked downhill to the stream, intending to strip off my clothes and climb into the warm pool where Padmasambhava used to soak. However, when I neared it, I saw the naljorpa on the other side. He walked upstream, and then turned and looked over his shoulder as if wanting me to follow. Was he going back to his cave?

"Hey, wait," I shouted, crossing the footbridge to catch up. When I looked upstream, he was gone. The thought of immersing myself in the stream disappeared, and I continued uphill. I wanted to ask him more about what had happened that morning. Had he really been there beside me, or was he only in my mind? Perhaps it was from him I was to receive the teachings that Saint Germain wanted made available in the West?

I continued following him uphill as the mountains closed in on either side. There was no place he could go other than straight ahead up the trail. Nearing the top of a ridge, well past the turnoff for his cave, I saw him again far ahead, ascending a trail that turned up the mountain on the left. Where was he going? I thought that for a man who it seemed didn't eat and walked barefoot on jagged rocks, he moved as quickly as a mountain goat.

A couple of hours later, a small, run-down monastery appeared ahead, and I felt drawn toward it as by a magnet. When I arrived, I found the gate open. Walking inside, the courtyard was empty, so I followed the sound of drums, trumpets, and the clashing of heavy cymbals, to the heavy wooden door of the shrine room. I was hesitant to enter and disturb the ritual. It might be some practice forbidden to outsiders, or for which some initiation was required, but as I stood there I felt that I must have been led there for a reason. I pushed the door open and went inside.

Instead of entering unnoticed at the back, as would have been the case if I were entering a church, I found myself in front of a gathering of monks. They sat at benches on the left and right that faced the center, and I stood there before them. At the opposite end of the temple sat a large golden statue of Padmasambhava, and below him the high lama beckoned me to enter. Although I was shocked to find myself standing in the center of this ritual, not a monk looked up from his text, nor did the beating of drums hesitate. I wanted to turn and exit, but felt rooted to the stone floor. Overcoming my fear, I realized I was supposed to prostrate. My American education shouted, "All beings are created equal, so never bow to anyone." Yet, my Higher Self took over and I threw myself face down on the floor, arms stretched overhead, as I had seen pilgrims do before the Jokhang temple in Lhasa. I felt an unexpected sense of satisfaction, as though certain blockages had been removed that allowed the spiritual energy to flow throughout my body. Then I stood up, motionless, wondering what to do next.

As if in answer to my uncertainty, a monk at a bench on the left side beckoned to a vacant cushion beside him. As I sat down, a young monk, no more than a boy, appeared with a cup of yak butter tea that he placed before me. As I took a sip of the hot, salty liquid, suddenly there was a blast of two eighteen-foot-long horns. Trumpets made from human thighbones sounded unexpectedly, accompanied by a clash of cymbals and throbbing drums, and I felt all rational thought processes dissolving. As a thought arose, it dissipated. Another thought tried to arise, but it too dissipated like a bubble pricked by a pin. Then no thoughts arose. Somehow the Tibetans had discovered how the mind worked. A thousand years ago, without scientific laboratories, they had found sounds that flattened the waves of repetitive thought. All analytical brain function ceased, leaving only mindfulness.

Suddenly the mantra began, a hundred monks chanting the Sanskrit words that Padmasambhava had said would produce enlightenment if done with focus and dedication:

Om Ah Hung Vajra Guru Padma Siddhi Hung.

As they chanted over and over I joined in, and felt the spirit coming more fully into my body. As my eyes were closing, the naljorpa who had given me the slip earlier suddenly slid onto the adjacent cushion. As I turned in awe, he deflected my attention from him to the statue of Padmasambhava, whom Buddhists call Guru Rinpoche (the guru that is a precious jewel). Then he tapped his finger on my chest and said, "God, guru, self, all one."

Then he took the mala from around his neck and, holding a bead between his thumb and forefinger, began chanting. With each repetition, he advanced another bead of the mala.

Focusing on the guru as an aspect of myself, that the living Padmasambhava was seated before me, yet that his consciousness and mine were one, I continued chanting. The formerly inert statue seemed to come to life, and energy from his body seemed to penetrate my being. As I heard the sound *Om,* a beam of white light shot from his forehead into mine, and the Sanskrit symbol of that word appeared in the center of my head. Rays of light emanated from that *Om* into limitless space for the benefit of all sentient beings.

Next came the sound *Ah,* as a beam of ruby light activated my throat center, and its symbol appeared also, radiating rays of red light. This was followed by *Hung,* with a blue light flowing from Guru Rinpoche's heart to my heart. That sapphire blue Sanskrit letter arose in my heart, radiating blue light into space, and my heart filled with compassion.

The form of Guru Rinpoche grew brighter, gradually becoming a being of pure light. Rays of wisdom, empowerment, and compassion radiated without limit. Then his form dissolved into a golden orb, and that orb entered my heart.

"Oh, I AM Guru Rinpoche," I gasped, finally realizing what the naljorpa meant by his assertion that God, guru, and self, are one. Not only my self, but everyone else's self are God and guru, the universal guru that is everywhere, and is called the precious jewel.

The room fell silent, almost shocking after the unremitting noise of the drums, horns, and cymbals. I turned to ask the naljorpa what to expect next, but he was gone, perhaps slipping out while my eyes were closed. I got up, hoping I would find him outside and follow him back to his cave, but when I left the monastery there was no trace of him. I wanted to talk to him about these tantric practices, and find out what had happened in the shrine room of the nunnery that morning. However, having passed out earlier, I did not want to risk hiking in the mountains, trying to find his cave. I was hungry, so I began my trek back down the rugged path, hoping we still had a good supply of tsampa.

Om Ah Hung

Chapter 10

Taking Refuge

W hen I returned to the convent and told Steve where I had been, and the mysterious naljorpa I had encountered, he said, "Oh, that sounds like Shunyata Dorje (Emptiness Thunderbolt), except he took a vow of silence twenty years ago."

When I described his appearance and the location of his cave, he said, "That's certainly him, because no other yogis live near there. The serious yogis live on the other side of the mountain, and never come over to this side. The tourist energy is not to their liking."

He continued, "If you are serious about Buddhism and are going to attend more practices, you will need to complete *ngondro,* the preliminary practices. At least that way you won't make a fool of yourself. However, before I can teach you that, you'll need to take refuge."[22]

"I think I took refuge from a lama who visited Mount Shasta years ago," I said, remembering that before giving the Green Tara empowerment, he had asked us to recite some lines in Tibetan.[23] To commit to

---

[22] Taking refuge does not mean seeking seclusion, but the process of committing to the Buddhist path of awakening symbolized by the Three Jewels: the Buddha, Dharma, and Sangha. The Buddha is a mirror of one's own awakened nature, the Dharma is the body of the teachings and their practice, and the Sangha is the company of other awakened beings who reinforce one's practice.

[23] The Green Tara is one of the twenty-one feminine aspects of enlightened mind. She represents success in undertakings, especially the pursuit of liberation. She is called

a religion made me nervous, as I remembered when I was in high school and a minister had tricked me into becoming a Presbyterian by forcing me to recite the Apostles Creed that stated I believed Jesus was the only son of God, that he had died for my sins, and now sat on the right hand of the Father. Later, I had a similar forced conversion when the Indian kid who called himself Guru Maharajji had tricked me into swearing loyalty to him. (For the whole story read *Search for the Guru: Adventures of a Western Mystic, Vol. I*).

Steve tried to allay my fears by saying, "You are not swearing allegiance to a person or a church, only to the process of awakening. It would be better if you took refuge with your root lama, but since you don't have a root lama, and since I have done the three-year retreat and am technically a lama, I can give you refuge."

Steve had been a surfer in the late 60s, living happily with his girlfriend in Maui, when a Tibetan lama arrived and gave a talk on how to escape suffering. Since he was leading the good life, he did not to want to hear about suffering, but his girlfriend liked the teachings. She also liked the lama, and left Maui with him. Then Steve's life of surfing turned into one of suffering, and he had an opportunity to apply the new

---

the Mother of all Buddhas and the Savioress who eliminates suffering. It is said that in a past life as Yeshe Dawa (Moon of Primordial Awareness), she was meditating, when some monks approached her and said that she would make greater progress if she re-embodied as a man. Infuriated, she vowed that not only would she achieve liberation as a woman, but also that she would remain in embodiment as a woman until the end of all samsara (illusion).

teachings. He began studying Buddhism, as well as other spiritual teachings, for now he needed to not only heal his heart, but also overcome his resentment of the lama who took his girlfriend.

Soon after losing his girlfriend, his father died, and he had enough money to travel the world in search of truth. He went from country to country over the next year, searching for someone who could help alleviate his feeling of emptiness. Eventually, in South India he found himself at the ashram of Sathya Sai Baba. After a long wait in the sweltering sun, Sai Baba approached him and said, "I am not your teacher. Your teacher is Tibetan, and you will find him in one year."

Exactly a year later to the day, he had an audience with the Sixteenth Karmapa, who told Steve that he had been expecting him. The Karmapa gave him refuge and, after completing the preliminary ngondro, he began a three-year retreat. During that time, the practices he was given helped transform his anger into equanimity, wisdom, and compassion. He also learned enough Tibetan so that eventually he could earn a living as a guide in Tibet.

He now explained that refuge was not hiding from anything, but fully embracing life so you could see the polarities of consciousness, the light within the dark, the fullness within the emptiness, the good within the bad, so you could awake to the true nature of reality. You take refuge, not from life, but from ignorance. You vow to seek awakening through the Three Jewels, symbolized by the Buddha (fully awakened consciousness), the Dharma (the teachings and practice), and the Sangha (association with others on the same path). The Sangha also includes other awakened beings, Buddhas and Bodhisattvas (what in the West would be called the Great White Brotherhood).[24] In other words, you are committing fully to the path of enlightenment.

"Let's start at the beginning, how to do prostrations," Steve continued.

"Oh, yes, I just did a prostration at the monastery."

"Good, you only have 99,999 left."

"What!"

"The first part of the preliminary practices is to do 100,000 prostrations, and each one includes a visualization and two prayers, one prayer on the way down, another on the way up."

Immediately, I saw the Presbyterian and Hindu inductions as mere inconveniences compared with this Buddhist practice. It got even worse when he said, "That's only the beginning. There are three more parts to this preliminary practice called *ngondro,* and you need to do each of them 100,000 times."

I was not excited about doing this ngondro, but I thought it would be good to at least learn how to do

---

[24] "The Great White Brotherhood" is a term that first appeared in 1925 in *The Masters and the Path* by C. W. Leadbeater, an early member of the Theosophical Society. However, this term is a misnomer, as the etheric Masters who are its members are both male and female. Nor do they consider themselves great. White refers to both the light they emit and the color of the robes in which they often appear, not to their race. A better name might be "Council of Light," a term used by the eighteenth century Bavarian writer Karl von Eckartshausen.

prostrations correctly, in case I participated in more Buddhist rituals.

"First of all," Steve began, "don't do this as an exercise. It's a practice that in itself can bring about enlightenment. Before enlightenment, however, comes humility, and the cultivation of that humility is one of the primary purposes of this practice. You are not demonstrating to the Buddha how humble you are by throwing yourself at his feet, but eliminating the arrogance of the ego by forcing it to acknowledge there is something higher than itself. It is the ego that you are forcing to bow in submission to your own Buddha Nature. As you do the practice, you may find all kinds of negative thoughts arising, like impatience, frustration, and anger. All these are the activity of the ego as it struggles to maintain its hold. Let everything arise; observe it, and then let it go. Gradually, all that will remain will be equanimity.

"Now, imagine a tree in front of you full of Buddhas. The roots are the roots of your consciousness, immersed in the ground of absolute reality. The trunk gives rise to individual Buddhas, who are manifestations of that consciousness. On each branch is another Buddha, so the whole tree represents all the lineages, enlightened teachers, and their teachings. In the New Age, this tree might be called the Hierarchy or the Great White Brotherhood. Of course, in the end, the whole tree dissolves into light, and you realize that you are the tree and all it contains.

"You are not doing these prostrations by yourself, but with hundreds, even thousands of other beings. On your left is your mother and all your female relatives, living and dead, and on your right is your father and all your male relatives, living and dead; without your relatives you would not be here. Your friends are there, too, standing behind you, and also your business associates and casual acquaintances. All world leaders are there, too. They are all in the space around you. In front of you are those who oppose you and make life challenging, what some call enemies."

"What! Why would I want to meditate on enemies? I thought we were trying to generate good energy here!" I exclaimed.

"Well, just think about who has taught you the most in life, friends or enemies? You learn a great deal from your enemies, so you want to honor them and pray for their evolution."

"Wow, I guess so."

"Even if you haven't learned from your enemies, they still have basic goodness. They act out of ignorance because they have not yet realized their goodness or that of others. Your visualization will help them realize their true nature, as well as help you realize your own. This will also protect you, as their negative energy will be repelled by your love. Now, here are the prayers you recite while prostrating."

"What! While I'm prostrating, you expect me to visualize a tree full of Buddhas, thousands of people around me, and say prayers too?"

"Well, if it was easy, everyone would be enlightened, wouldn't they?" Steve laughed. "Here's the first prayer you say as you are prostrating:

From now until I become fully enlightened,
I take refuge in the guru who is the embodiment
of the Three Jewels.

"Hold your palms together and raise them over your head; then bring them down with fingers touching your lips, and finally bring the palms down to your heart. Then kneel and put your hands on the floor. Slide forward, face to the ground, arms stretched all the way forward toward the Buddha Tree, offering every aspect of yourself to enlightenment."

I prostrated as he instructed, attempting to surrender my ego, and to my surprise I felt a great sense of satisfaction. I lay face down, immersed in surrender. I felt my sense of self was gone, until Steve jolted me with the reminder, "You had everyone else prostrate along with you, right?"

"Not exactly."

"Well, imagine that they did prostrate and are lying there face down with you. Now, here is the second prayer to recite as you get up:

From now until all beings have attained liberation, I will bring about benefit and happiness for all beings that have been my mothers.

"Wait a minute, Steve, how many beings is that?"

"Everyone. Also all animals, even worms."

"That's a bit of a stretch, isn't it? You think that ant over there, crawling across the shrine room floor, has been my mother?"

"In terms of infinity, which is what we're dealing with, that ant either has been or will be your mother, so should be treated accordingly."

"I'm sorry, I don't believe that ant has ever been, or will ever be, my mother."

"Well, scientists are discovering that all the stuff of which the universe is composed is recycled, that our bodies are made of the stuff of stars that burned out eons ago. Even the particles of Napoleon's body are still being recycled and may be a part of us now, and someday they will be used to create a future sun. So, why can't that ant be at least part of someone who was, or will be, your mother? If you see everyone you meet as the embodiment of your mother, you will treat them differently, won't you?"

"Okay, I get your point. I'll give it a try."

"Now, get up. But, while you are rising, keep in mind the Buddha tree, as well as all the others with you, and recite the prayer. At the end, bring your hands together in prayer over your heart. Congratulations, you have done a prostration. When you finish all 100,000 let me know, and I'll give you the next part."

"Isn't there a shortcut, Steve? This will take forever."

"It will be forever, if you don't finish in this lifetime and have to come back again. Get busy and do them as if your life depended on it, and you can finish them in three and a half months."

Steve left and I began right away. However, at that altitude I felt light-headed after only 25 prostrations and had to stop, as I didn't want to pass out again. I had worked up a sweat, so I went down to the stream to sit on Padmasambhava's rock.

As I was soaking in the hot water, contemplating the prospect of doing another 99,975 prostrations, I felt Saint Germain's presence. He said quite clearly, "Peter, you already completed the prostrations in a past life and no longer need to do them. The humility you gained is a part of you. However, this is a practice that would benefit many New Agers who take courses in spirituality and soon proclaim themselves teachers, or who begin channeling whatever thoughts come into their mind, claiming that it is coming from a Master. Those are the ones who should do prostrations to get beyond the grip of the ego."

His etheric form faded and I breathed a sigh of relief. I relaxed into the warm mineral water swirling around my body, and sank into a natural meditation. Inwardly, I felt

I am consciousness pervading all space.

As that awareness flowed outward, my being filled with joy. Gradually, I came back into body awareness and looked down. I almost expected to see the water bubbling with effervescence as I heard that it did in the Ascended Master retreats, but it was simply swirling past.

As I walked back up the hill, I decided not to tell Steve of the reprieve, although I would still prostrate when entering temples. In fact, I found it satisfying to stretch out face down, stretch my arms overhead toward the Buddha, and feel the ordinary self disappear. I began to feel that a single prostration done with full intent might equal a hundred done unconsciously. I later realized that a prostration done in meditation before the living Buddha, who is one with the I AM Presence, was equally effective. The essence of tantra, however, is to have the awareness of meditation in daily life. Life is the meditation. We can prostrate at any moment, wherever we are, and without anyone knowing. We can prostrate inwardly before everyone we meet, making every encounter sacred, and an opportunity for growth.

Pilgrims prostrating on way to Lhasa

Chapter 11

Your Three Bodies

We left Tidrum the next day. After driving for a couple of hours, we came upon a group of pilgrims walking single file by the side of the road. Every third step, each one prostrated in the dirt. They had boards strapped to each hand so that when they slid forward the gravel would not lacerate their palms. Their foreheads had red sores from the repeated banging.

"Where are they headed, Steve?" I asked.

"Lhasa, to prostrate at the Jokhang Temple."

"Why that's over two hundred miles! How long will that take them?"

"Several months, but they don't view time like we do. What is a two-month pilgrimage out of lifetimes spent wandering in samsara?"

"Well, Steve, you won't get many westerners to sign up for that workshop!"

"No, not many would sign up," he replied, "but how many Americans get enlightened attending workshops? The teachings we need are already available, but few apply them. People want instant results. It's much easier to sit around listening to channeled messages saying that you are already a Master. In the old days, before a Master would give teachings, you would have to go on a pilgrimage, or at least finish your prostrations."

I thought of the yogi I had met in India who had spent twenty years meditating on the side of a mountain, and also the meditation teacher for the Ramakrishna Mission I had met who knew over five hundred types of meditation. Then I thought of the girl I met from Berkeley, California. She had taken a workshop on meditation and then started advertising herself as a meditation instructor.

We finally arrived at a monastery which required a long hike uphill. When we arrived, I was out of breath, and sat down in the back of the main shrine room to rest. As I sat gazing at the statues of mahasiddhas who had been great teachers, I noticed a thangka on the front wall and felt the inner prompting to look closer. I saw that the central figure was Padmasambhava, yet my attention was drawn to two figures, one above the other, seated over his head. A monk who saw my interest came over. With a kind smile, he pointed to the middle figure, "This Chenrezig, Lord of Compassion."

Then he pointed to the top figure that was surrounded in an aura of rainbow light, "This one Amitabha Buddha, Lord of Infinite Light."

I suddenly realized that I was looking at the ancient Tibetan version of the chart of the I AM Presence. Amitabha Buddha, Lord of Infinite Light, was the I AM Presence *(Dharmakaya)*. Chenrezig, the Lord of Compassion, represented the soul or Higher Mental Body *(Sambogakaya)*. Padmasambhava represented the *Nirmanakaya*, the physical body of the yogi. All three bodies were connected by a cord of light that descended from the top figure down to the heart of the bottom one, yet each being was doing individual work at its own level.

Padmasambhava was pointing to a golden sun in the center of his chest, in which was written the Sanskrit letter *Hung*, the indweller of the heart (Sanskrit: *Hridayavasi*). From that letter emanated myriad rays of rainbow colored light. Surrounding it was a six-pointed star representing the union of heaven and earth, the union of the feminine and masculine consciousness.

This is where Saint Germain had long ago said to focus my energy. It is here that the surrender of the human ego to Divine Will occurs, and it is also here where one feels guidance in the moment; the spontaneous, correct action that is the key to mastery. It is also only in the heart that one develops compassion, the lack of which impels one to an endless cycle of rebirths. Even though illusion is penetrated with the mind and meditation on that center is important, without bringing that consciousness to the heart one's achievement remains purely mental. That light in the heart is like the pilot light of a gas stove; although not visible, it is burning all the time. When activated, it illuminates all the other chakras.

Continuing to admire the tapestry, I realized that Saint Germain had simplified this elaborate representation of our three-fold being into the version he inspired May DaCamera to paint for Mr. Ballard. When he saw it, he said that a copy should hang in every home as a constant reminder of our true identity.

When Steve found me, I explained what I had observed about the three-fold body portrayed in the thangka. He said that the Tibetans have practices that develop awareness of these higher bodies, but the teachings are rarely given to westerners, who want instant results and are unwilling to spend time on mastering the practices. As most of the enlightened lamas have died, this ancient wisdom is being lost. The new lamas may have studied the texts and completed three-year retreats, but have not had the necessary enlightened tutelage to achieve selfless awareness.

As we left the monastery and walked down toward the car, I visualized my higher bodies. I imagined my Higher Mental Body as a luminous Christ hovering above me, and ready to help at any time. Higher yet was the sun-like God Presence, the source of my being, surrounded by rainbow light. A cord of blue-white light descended from the I AM Presence to my Christ Self, and then continued down through the top of my head to the center of my chest—the Unfed Flame. As I walked, a surge of energy confirmed its presence within. I knew from years of practicing heart-centered meditation with Pearl, that by stilling the mind and tuning in to this Unfed Flame in the center of the chest, you can feel its unwavering guidance.

It is the awareness and expansion of that energy within every cell that leads to the ascension, the attainment of the Rainbow Body—a process that can only be completed after all egotism and clinging to the human self has been dissolved. As long as there is the slightest desire to profit at the expense of another, or any feeling of superiority, one returns again and again into physical rebirth to learn whatever lesson still remains.[25]

---

[25] I would like to distinguish between the attainment of the rainbow body (Tibetan: *jalus)* and what many western students of esotericism call ascension. In the former case, the yogi consciously dissolves the physical body and merges the higher bodies with the I AM Presence. In the later, which takes place after death, the soul achieves the same union with the I AM Presence. There is also a state of liberation known in India as *moksha,* where the soul has purified its

As we drove across the seemingly endless Tibetan plateau, I used a simple method Steve taught, the Six Nails of Tilopa, to still my mind.

- Let go of the past.
- Let go of the future.
- Let go of the present and whatever you think is happening.
- Don't try to understand anything.
- Don't try to make anything happen.
- Relax, and be aware of now.

I began to feel that I didn't really need to do anything, that Mastery was not in using the will to make things happen, so much as getting the mind out of the way so that what was meant to happen could come forth unimpeded.

---

karma and is free from the desire to re-embody on earth in human form. This decision not to re-embody on Earth takes place on what is known in the West as Judgment Day, the time when each departed soul, under the guidance of a Master, reviews its past lifetimes and sees what remains to be learned, if anything.

Padmasambhava's three bodies

Chapter 12

Stopping for a Beer

After a long time driving on the dusty roads, we came to a crossroads where there was a hut with a thatched roof.

"What's that?" I asked.

" A place that serves beer; want to try some?" Steve replied.

I was thirsty after the long drive, and although I rarely drank alcohol, yet thought it would be a shame to drive past without trying the famous Tibetan drink made of fermented barley known as *chang*. We pulled off the road and walked into the small enclosure made of grass mats lashed to poles, and a toothless old lady greeted us with a smile and waved for us be seated. There were no tables, so we sat on the dirt floor, leaning against the poles that held the place together. Soon she emerged from the back with a large cup in each hand.

I looked down into the amber liquid and, noticing sprouted barley floating on the surface, asked Steve, "What else is in here?"

"Probably some aconite," Steve said, looking wistfully into the murky liquid.

"Aconite!" I exclaimed, knowing from studying Chinese medicine that aconite was toxic, and that it needed to be mixed with other herbs to derive a healing rather than fatal effect.

"Every once in a while you hear of someone dying from *chang*, but I'm sure this place is OK."

I wasn't so sure, as the hut had no running water or washroom, and the woman who served this home brew looked like the Goddess of Death. The cups were probably never washed, except rinsed with water and dried on the matron's apron.

I prayed for guidance,

Saint Germain, please protect me from doing anything I shouldn't do, and blaze the violet flame up, in, around, and through this drink, dissolving and consuming anything less than perfection.

"Life is impermanent, and you're going to die soon anyway," Steve volunteered some a basic Buddhist truism.

"Thanks, Steve. Here's to impermanence," I said, toasting a favorite Buddhist concept, and took a sip.

I was surprised to find the drink one of the most refreshing, yet nourishing, drinks I had ever consumed. It seemed alive, imparting the feeling that in this beverage I was drinking the essence of Tibet and its dharma. The spirit of the drink came from the same land where Vajrayana had taken root twelve hundred years ago.

After a few sips, it occurred to me that I still didn't know the rest of the preliminary practices, so I asked Steve about the other three parts of the ngondro.

"You have to do the Vajrasattva mantra!" he said, with a gleam in his eye.

"Who is Vajrasattva?"

"The God who creates all the other Gods."

"What—how is that possible?" I asked. My Christian conditioning said that there is only one God.

"God is only a concept. God is a form that people impose on limitless awareness. Out of that limitless consciousness, which you can call Buddhahood, beings arise who embody all its qualities. Those beings take on denser and denser forms for their own growth and evolution, and manifest other beings like themselves; and here we are. We, too, are Buddhas and Christs, whatever name you want to call awakened awareness. Vajrasattva is simply one of those Buddhas of which the others are a reflection. Jesus himself said,

> *You are created in the image and likeness of God.*

"So, too, are we. Jesus didn't say he was God, only that he and the Father were one. We, too, are one with the Father, only I choose to call him Vajrasattva. He said,

> *May anyone be purified entirely of their harmful past actions merely by hearing my name, thinking of me, or reciting my mantra. Furthermore, may I remain in embodiment until all beings are purified.*

"Wow, that's an amazing vow. What's the mantra?"

"It has a hundred syllables, and you need to repeat it a hundred thousand times."

"What!" I exclaimed. "Why does everything Buddhist need a hundred thousand repetitions?"

"I suppose if you could do it with total awareness, you would only need to repeat it once, but then you would probably already be enlightened. All I know is that this method works. The Tibetans have been doing it this way for over a thousand years, and many have achieved the Rainbow Body. How many New Agers have ascended by going to abundance workshops, listening to psychics, or searching for their twin rays?"

I realized that the only person I knew who had ascended was my teacher, Pearl, and she did it after death. Not even her teacher, Godfre Ray King, had been able to dematerialize his physical body.

"Ok, what's the mantra?"

"Sorry, I can't teach you that while drinking beer."

We finished our chang and stood to leave. After paying and thanking the lady who had served us, we walked to the car to continue our journey to Lhasa. I looked out over the vast plains where not a single car had passed during the time we had been inside. We were at a major crossroads where two roads intersected, one coming from the North, the other from the East, seeming to be symbolic of the need to assimilate this eastern path of consciousness with the western path of activity in the world.

As we drove, I still wanted to know the other two parts of the preliminary practice. Since there was nothing else to do for a few hours except to try and generate inner heat whenever Lobsang lowered the window, I asked Steve what those practices were.

"You have to offer up all your possessions—not only what you have now, but everything you have ever owned in all your lifetimes, and whatever you might own in the future. In fact, you have to offer up the entire universe. Then you recreate it, offering the new universe for the benefit of all sentient beings. It's a practice you do with a pile of grain, coins, and the most precious gems you can gather, which you pour over a metal pan that represents the ocean of awareness."

"Let me guess, I have to do it a hundred thousand times?"

"Exactly."

"What comes after I have recreated the universe?"

"Guru yoga. You visualize Padmasambhava in front of you as you recite his mantra. Finally, he dissolves into light and merges with you. Isn't that what happened at the monastery above Tidrum?"

"Wow, every one of these rituals seems to involve merging with a God!"

"Yes, in that way you become a God. But, it is not just saying, 'I AM God,' which can lead to ego centered awareness. To actually awaken to God, you must learn to step outside your ego, and by seeing it clearly, transform it. Most New Age teachings lead to self-cherishing, strengthening the ego's tendency to self-worship and control others, when it is that attachment to the illusory self that needs to be dissolved."

"You remember Milarepa, don't you," Steve asked, "the magician in the eleventh century who cast a spell on his aunt and uncle after they cheated him and his mother out of their home at his father's death?"

"Oh yes, wasn't he the one whose guru had him build a rock tower on a cliff and after he was finished told him that he had built it in the wrong place, then had him put the rocks back and build another tower in a new location?"

"Exactly, and three more towers, each one having to be deconstructed for some seemingly frivolous reason. Yet, his guru, Marpa, had a reason for inflicting these ordeals. He saw that he needed to reduce Milarepa to total despair nine times to expiate the karma for the people he had injured and killed through his magic, before he would be ready for initiation. However, after the eighth ordeal and close to suicide, instead Milarepa persuaded Marpa's wife to write him a letter of introduction to another guru who lived nearby. She forged her husbands name and seal—and Milarepa ran off to the new guru."

"I don't remember what happened there."

"Here, read this," said Steve, throwing me the book with the frayed cover I'd seen in his coat pocket since the beginning of the trip. "It's my bible. Whenever I get depressed, I read this and it reminds me that my suffering is only burning off some karma in preparation for further teaching."

I looked at the cover, *The Life of Milarepa* by Tsangnyön Heruka. I asked the I AM Presence to guide me to what I needed to read, and flipped the book open to the exact place describing Milarepa's arrival before his new guru, lama Ngokpa. The lama was reciting a tantric ritual in front of his students, and was saying:

> *I AM the Way.*
> *I AM the Truth.*
> *I AM the universal Teacher.*
> *I AM the Eternal Blissful One.*
> *I AM the World, and beyond the World.*

I was shocked, for here were affirmations similar to those of Jesus as well as Saint Germain:

> *I AM the Way, the Truth, and the Life.*
> *I AM the resurrection and the life.*
> *I AM one with the Father.*
> *I AM a Son of God.*

I realized that he was not saying these affirmations from ego, but from the state of ego-less awareness, in non-dual union with his Higher Self—the state of consciousness where attributes come forth into outer reality by claiming them as aspects of one's true nature.

It was only through these ordeals that Milarepa went through that he was prepared for advanced teachings. However, in fleeing from his guru with a forged letter, he had created new karma that he would also need to expiate, and which prevented him from being able to apply the new teachings from the second guru. He had to return to Marpa and suffer further before being ready for the initiation that finally led to enlightenment.

"Thanks, Steve, that was just what I needed to read," I said, handing the book back. "It seems that the stories of Jesus visiting Tibet and receiving these teachings from lamas must be true. Certainly, two thousand years ago no one in the Mediterranean was giving tantric teachings."

Chapter 13

It's Not Fair

From the beginning of the trip, Steve and I had been aware that Betty was not happy with the way things were working out. She did not function well without a plan. She never knew what to expect. Despite her effort at pretending to be serene, her anger finally erupted in a volcanic explosion.

"It's not fair!" she shouted.

I turned around to see her trembling with rage. Steve, who was sitting beside her, turned to face this newly arisen demon. "What isn't fair?" he asked.

"It's not fair how I've been treated. You spent a half hour drinking with Peter and left me in the car."

"But, I invited you to join us," Steve said.

"Yes, but in the last monastery, you and Peter went off to talk Buddhism, and left me to wander around alone."

"But, you never showed any interest; you said Buddhism was superstition and the worship of false Gods."

"Still, I have been ignored the whole time," Betty pouted.

"I'm so sorry you feel that way," Steve replied. "I wonder if there is anything we can do for you?"

"Yes, there is. We can turn around and go home!"

Steve instructed Lobsang to stop the car. We coasted to a halt in the middle of the highway and Lobsang turned off the engine. We blocked the road, but it didn't really seem to matter. Steve struggled to maintain his view of seeing all phenomena as empty of ultimate meaning.

"It's just as long to go back as forward," Steve said. In my mind's eye, I saw the dusty roads that sometimes disappeared and went up riverbeds that we had traversed to get this far.

"Why don't we take a vote?" he said, relying on the American concept that everyone, no matter how stupid or uneducated, should be equally qualified to judge and vote on the merits of the most complex question. He concluded by saying that he would abstain from voting. He would vote only if Betty and I didn't agree.

Since Betty had already made her opinion clear, it was up to me. Sitting pensively for a moment, hoping that Betty would appreciate the consideration I was giving her request, and not wanting to trigger another outburst, I finally said, "I vote to continue."

"Since there is a tie, I vote to continue, also," Steve seconded.

Betty bit her lip. The knuckles of her clenched fists were white, yet she sat as immobile as a Buddha. Expecting her silence to end with an emotional explosion, I wondered if repression could be a form of meditation? Perhaps she realized all along that her request was ridiculous, but she just needed to express her stress. Karma settled back in her seat with a sigh, and Lobsang restarted the engine. Just then a huge truck carrying rock from one of the new Chinese mines barreled past, shaking the car with its wind. Had our car pulled away a half second sooner, we would have been obliterated.

As we drove, Betty's "It's not fair," echoed in my mind. The Chinese occupation of Tibet, the imprisonment and execution of lamas, and the destruction of their temples seemed also not fair.

However, even the Dalai Lama said that Tibet was reaping the seeds of its past actions. The feudal theocracy had become corrupt, with various sects fighting to consolidate their power. Many monasteries focused more on generating money than on practicing meditation. Many lamas knew that it was inner weakness that made invasion inevitable; and it was that invasion that drove them finally into the outer world to share their teachings.[26]

---

[26] On many previous occasions Tibetan nomads waged war against parts of China. As the result of a war by Tibetan king Songtsen Gampo against the Chinese Emperor of Tang, peace was brought about by his marriage to Princess Wencheng (628-680). This Chinese girl was the first to bring Buddhism to Central Tibet. She also brought with her an advanced understanding of agriculture, medicine, and art, and was largely responsible for the creation of the Tibetan alphabet. Today she is still revered by Tibetans as a compassionate embodiment of the Goddess Tara. Two centuries later, Padmasambhava brought Vajrayana Buddhism to Central Tibet from India, although it already existed in Western Tibet due to the teachings of a previous Buddha in Bhactria, present day Afghanistan.

Roof of the Potala Palace, Lhasa.

Chapter 14

Return to Lhasa

As we continued toward Lhasa, we eventually came to one of the new Chinese schools. These were clean, well-built structures for the education of the next generation of young Tibetans. The students were taught Chinese, which they would need to get a job in the new Communist society. They were forbidden from studying Buddhism, which they were told was superstition.

Since our translator spoke some Chinese, the administrator gave us a tour. Since we had arrived between classes, the eager faces of hundreds of young Tibetans greeted us. When the administrator turned to talk with a teacher, Steve whispered to the kids in Tibetan, and I suddenly found myself surrounded by kids clinging to my robe.

"Steve, what did you say?" I asked.

"I told them that you are an American *tulku* (reincarnated lama)," he said, smiling.[27]

---

[27] *Tulku,* the keeper of a particular teaching or lineage who re-embodies and is then discovered by his former associates or students. Usually the being leaves hints or clues as to where and when the rebirth should be sought. This practice began with the lineage of the Karmapas. Sometimes the correct soul is not found, perhaps because that being has ascended. Or, as has happened recently, the rediscovered being no longer wishes to be recognized. In a recent case, Osel Hita Torres (born in Barcelona, Spain, 1985) was recognized as a tulku soon after birth, but in 2009 announced his decision to instead become a filmmaker.

The administrator whirled around, shouting at the kids to get to their next class, and gave Steve a scowl that said we had better leave.

As we continued toward Lhasa, I could not get the open, smiling faces of the kids out of my mind, and was saddened that they were not at least being taught the Four Thoughts That Turn the Mind to the Dharma, that had been an intrinsic part of Tibetan Buddhist Culture for centuries. One contemplates:

- Precious life: To be alive in a human body is an extraordinary opportunity.
- Impermanence: Everything comes to an end, and death can come at any time.
- Karma: Every action has an effect. Our experiences of this life are the result of our past actions. Our present actions can nullify past karma and create positive future effects.
- Samsara: Clinging to worldly things that are constantly changing, including clinging to the illusory self, leads to suffering.

Instead of offering these basic contemplations that stimulate the desire for truth and liberation, they were being taught to pursue solely material wellbeing. I wished that I could have brought a few of these kids home, or at least found them homes with Dharma practitioners; but for now, I would have to be content with praying for their spiritual awakening.

We arrived in Lhasa by nightfall, and checked in to our hotel. Lobsang and Karma left to stay with their families. As Steve, Betty, and I were famished, we went out for dinner. Walking toward the Dharmaland Restaurant near the Jokhang Temple, we came to a young Tibetan man wielding a pickax, digging a hole in the sidewalk. He must have been ordered to make repairs, I thought, and I asked him, with Steve translating, "Are the Communists forcing you to work late?"

"No, they're not forcing me to do anything. I'm working hard so I can buy a stereo."

"That is the new generation," Steve said, "liberated from feudalism to become enslaved by materialism."

We soon reached the restaurant, and I scanned the menu. After days of fruit cup, biscuits, tsampa, and cabbage stuffed momos, I salivated at the thought of eating something more substantial. However, I was surprised to see that the menu was filled with international delicacies such as Chicken Marseilles, Hungarian Goulash, and Peking Duck.

"Where is the Tibetan food?" I asked the waiter.

"You mean what the peasants are eating right now, huddled in their huts?"

"Yes, exactly. This is Tibet, so I want to eat the local food."

"OK, you want authentic food, I bring it; but you order something else too."

Shortly a bowl of barley broth arrived, a few pieces of carrot and onion floating on the surface.

"Your authentic Tibetan dinner," the waiter said, placing the bowl on the table with a wry smile.

As there were no other vegetarian dishes, I followed his advice, and with some trepidation ordered Yak Teriyaki. After praying for the animal that had given its life, I noticed the high-quality protein restoring my body to life.

After dinner, I stood by the cash register waiting to pay, when I noticed a framed document on the wall that said, "Joint Venture Agreement."

"Joint venture with whom?" I asked the waiter.

"The Chinese government."

"Wow, how does that work?"

"Our family puts up the money and does all the work, and they get half the profits."

I wanted to ask more, but he signaled me to keep silent. I knew that if he were heard complaining, he risked imprisonment, so I nodded and dropped the subject.

On the walk back to the hotel, Betty dropped a few steps behind us, due to the narrow sidewalk, but after a couple of blocks, she suddenly pushed between us and blocked our path. Scowling, she shouted to Steve, "I'm fed up with you. You have been ignoring me through this whole tour. This is not the service I paid for. We did not get the food or accommodations promised in the brochure. The very least you can do, now that we are at the end of the tour, is put us up at the Holiday Inn for the last couple of nights!"

"I will see what I can do," Steve said, trying to avoid a scene in the street. However, the matter was soon going to be taken out of his hands. At the hotel, Chinese soldiers blocked the entrance. A plainclothes agent in a leather jacket herded us inside and checked our passports. Another agent with a pistol on his belt guarded the lobby. Behind the desk, the hotel owner said apologetically, "You are going to have to leave."

It seems that a United States senator on a secret fact-finding mission to investigate the Chinese treatment of Tibetans had stayed at the hotel while we were gone. His messages back to Washington had been intercepted, and the authorities were now closing the hotel as punishment. The senator was long gone, never realizing the hardship he caused the hotel owner and the employees, who now lost their jobs. I prayed to Saint Germain to take command, yet the Chinese agent still would not allow us to stay.

Betty was finally going to get her wish fulfilled of staying at the Holiday Inn, although the fulfillment of that wish would not turn out as pleasantly as she had hoped. Soon a taxi deposited us before the modern Holiday Inn facade, which all look the same throughout the world. I would have preferred to remain at the Tibetan hotel, yet the thought of a hot shower sounded good.

Chapter 15

At the Tibetan Medical and Astrological Institute

Our last day in Lhasa, we decided to go to the Tibetan Medical and Astrological Institute, *Men-Tsee-Lhang,* and have an appointment with one of their doctors. We had heard of their legendary skills in treating all types of physical as well as emotional and even spiritual conditions. The original course of study was fourteen years, the last half focusing on the curing of spiritual illnesses. Due to the shortage of doctors, the course had been shortened to seven years to treat the more critical physical conditions.

The walls of the waiting room were filled with thangkas portraying the principles on which their medicine was founded, and showing in graphic form all the unhealthy actions that caused the various conditions of ill health. These ranged from physical causes such as overwork, wrong diet, and exposure to toxins, to emotional toxins such as desire, anger, grief, pride, greed, and jealousy, to more etheric causes such as possession by earth-bound souls, giving offense to nature spirits, and planetary influences. Even geopathic causes were shown, such as living too close to water or where the land had been disturbed. Since there were no chairs, a patient had to walk around, and by viewing the pictures become educated about health. In that way, the doctor would not have to waste time explaining the cause of the illness, and could get on with the cure.

A young Tibetan woman in traditional dress soon escorted us into a small room, and an elderly man seated behind a desk greeted us. He smiled kindly and motioned us to sit. Steve whispered in my ear, "We're fortunate; this is the head doctor. He's quite famous. How old do you think he is?"

"At the most, sixty?"

"Ninety-two. Most of the doctors that were imprisoned during the invasion died, and he was one of the few that escaped prison and fled to India. He came back later to rebuild the institute. Supposedly he's the reincarnation of Yuthok, who wrote *Compassionate Sunlight for Dispersing Suffering's Darkness (Yuthok Nyingthik Guru Sadhana)* in the twelfth century, the main practice of the Medicine Buddha. In that life, he studied in India and brought Ayurveda back to Tibet, where it was combined with the Chinese medicine that had been imported in the seventh century by the Chinese empress Wencheng."

The eminent doctor took Betty's forearm between his fingers, gently feeling the six pulses in each wrist, three on the surface and three deeper, then looked at her tongue and peered into her eyes. Within a minute, he divulged her medical history as accurately as if reading her clinical records. He mentioned all her illnesses and surgeries, even telling her the year of her hysterectomy. He went on to explain her present health challenges.

"Never have surgery unless absolutely necessary," he emphasized. "It creates scar tissue that blocks the flow of energy. Many of your problems, even the emotional ones, are the result of blocked energy. This is the karmic result of injuries you inflicted on others in past lives. To overcome this, you must stop thinking about only yourself, and do something to help others. As you develop compassion, your health will improve.

In the meantime, I will give you some pills to strengthen your digestion."

Fixing her with a penetrating gaze, he said, "Do not eat dairy products or sweet desserts," then wrote a prescription for her to get filled downstairs at the dispensary.

Then he reached for my wrist, and I sensed his consciousness in each fingertip. His attention seemed to probe beyond the pulses to the very soul. I felt I was in the hands of a Master. After fifteen seconds of silence, he said, "There is nothing wrong with you that won't improve when you return to a lower altitude. You are in excellent health, will live a long life, and will help many people."

He then opened a drawer and pulled out what appeared to be a marble wrapped in blue silk, tied closed with rainbow-colored threads. He casually placed the mysterious object in my hand and said, "Here is the Most Precious Wish-Fulfilling Jewel *(Rinchen Ratna Samphel),*" the very object I had been seeking. It was to obtain this that the Karmapa had sent me to Tibet.

I was speechless as I continued to stare at the ornately wrapped sphere in the palm of my hand. I thought that it would be given to me by a yogi in the mountains, or perhaps by a lama at the end of a long empowerment. Now a doctor handed it to me with no more ceremony than an aspirin. He smiled and stood, indicating that the interview was over. At the door, I thanked him profusely for the jewel, but he simply nodded. I did not want the session to end, with this amazing man who had fulfilled at least part of my mission. To prolong the contact, I asked if he still had resentment about being imprisoned by the Chinese.

"No regrets," he said, calmly. "While in prison I met a great doctor, and from him I learned many secret healing methods. I am grateful for that time with him that I would not have had if I had not been in prison."

I thanked him again for the Wish-Fulfilling Jewel, which I now put in my pocket, and we went downstairs to the dispensary to help Betty get her medicine. Waiting before the dispensary window, I heard chanting coming from down the hall. Following it, I entered an elaborate shrine room, where dozens of monks were performing a ceremony. Bags of herbal medicine pills that they had made by hand were placed before the shrine, and I realized they were doing the Medicine Buddha practice to charge the pills with healing consciousness. Soon the chanting of the Sanskrit mantra began,

Tayata Om Bekandze, Bekandze,
Mahabekandze, Ratza Samundgate Swaha.

(Tay-a-taa Om Beck-an-zay, Beck-an-zay, Maha Beck-an-zay, Raatza Samund-got-ay Swa-ha).

Feeling the energy, I realized that much of the healing power of the medicine came, not just from their constituent herbs and minerals, but more from what they charged into the medicine. Steve said that the mantra translates as an invocation to remove suffering—even the cause and memory of suffering— to purify the person to merge with the body, speech, and mind of this Buddha.

We did not have time to stay for the entire ritual, but Steve said that the ritual would conclude, like other tantric practices, with the visualization of the Deity dissolving into the medicine pills, as well as merging into each of the monks. I later realized that in these practices, once one deciphers the Tibetan, one usually finds a statement similar to,

I AM the Deity.

However, to avoid the trap of the ego claiming to be God, that affirmation is said only after first attaining the egoless state of samadhi. Furthermore, at the end of the ritual the visualization is dissolved, and one does not rise from the floor until first returning to normal awareness. Hence, one does not walk around in a state of feeling superior to anyone. These practices are also given out only to those who have at least begun their ngondro practice and who are also doing the compassion practice of *tonglen*. If one starts feeling superior, or that their compassion for others is diminishing instead of increasing, they have not truly understood the path.

After Betty received her packet of medicine, we left the clinic and headed back toward the hotel. I felt the blue *Ratna Samphel* in my pocket, and then realized that I had not been charged for the jewel-like pill. Perhaps I had generated enough good karma to receive this blessing, after treating so many people at my naturopathic clinic in Mount Shasta without charge.

As this was our last night in Lhasa, I agreed to meet Betty in the dining room of the Holiday Inn for dinner. At the smorgasbord, I heaped my plate with the steaming vegetables I had been craving during our journey. As we dined, I tried to ignore her complaints about Steve and the tour company, which she was now threatening to sue for misrepresentation. After we finished eating, I was surprised when Betty went to the dessert table and selected a couple of creampuffs.

"I wouldn't eat those if I were you," I cautioned, "Remember what the doctor said this morning."

"Oh, this is the Holiday Inn," she said, seeming confident that the western aura of cleanliness would protect her from harm. Yet, the next morning when we met in the lounge, her face had a greenish hue and she had stomach pains. As we waited by the door for Lobsang to arrive with the car to take us to the airport, she said she had vomited during the night and now had a fever.

White Tara

Chapter 16

Appearance of the Divine Mother

As we approached the Lhasa airport to board our return flight to Kathmandu, Steve mentioned that since the tour company only paid Lobsang and Karma a minimal wage, it would be nice if Betty and I would give them a gratuity. Betty reacted swiftly, saying she had already been overcharged.

I took out my wallet and found that I still had about fifty dollars in Chinese Renmebi, so I stuffed half in each of the two envelopes Steve offered. When we got out of the car at the airport, Steve handed one envelope to Karma and the other to Lobsang.

Both bowed, raising their clasped hands to their foreheads in gratitude. I turned to pick up my bag, and Karma stepped forward and placed in my hand a small picture of the White Tara, the Goddess embodying wisdom, purity, healing, and longevity. Touched by her kindness, I bowed in return, holding the picture above the crown of my head as Tibetans do when showing reverence for a sacred object.

"She will watch over you," Karma said. "I have been watching you on this trip, and I see you are good man. You want to help others. I do White Tara practice and have been praying to her for you. Say her mantra and she will help you:

Om Tare Tuttare Ture Mama Ayuh Punya Jñana Pustim Kuru Svaha

(Om Tare' Too-tare' Mama Aye-you Pun-ya Gyana Pootim Kuru Swaha)

At that moment, I saw the etheric form of white-robed Tara above Karma, sending down rays of white light into my heart. During the entire trip, I had not asked her about her spiritual practice, and realized now how intense her devotion and visualization must be. I felt deeply humbled that she had been moved to include me in her mandala and call forth this blessing. I put my palms together in prayer and gratitude to Karma, and to her Higher Self as Tara.

The car pulled away from the curb, and I waved goodbye to these two kind people who had been my driver and translator, then picked up my backpack and entered the airport. I felt that Tibet and her people had given me much to share when I returned to the West.

In Lhasa on March 10, 2008, a group shouting "Free Tibet" in the main square in front of the Jokhang Temple was fired upon by Chinese soldiers. Approximately 500 Tibetans died, Karma apparently one of them. Lobsang, although not a protestor, was likely imprisoned in Drepung Monastery for "re-education," along with about 5,000 other Tibetans. His fate is unknown.

Chapter 17

Betty's Transformation

Once inside the airport, Betty's condition worsened. Barely able to walk, she stumbled back and forth to the bathroom. Steve was concerned that they might not let her board the plane. To make matters worse, our flight was delayed an hour. To pass the time, I went into a corner of the waiting room and began to practice *Tai Chi*. After I'd done a few moves, two Chinese guards approached with rifles. They were a male and female, neither of whom could have been much over eighteen.

"Stop! What are you doing?" the boy asked.

"Yes, what is that?" the girl added, watching with curiosity.

"Tai Chi."

"American?"

"No, Chinese! You've never seen it before?"

They shook their heads, perplexed, and walked away. I was astounded. In the two generations since the Cultural Revolution, the Communists had eliminated all knowledge of a health practice that had been part of the Chinese culture for millennia. Although the guards hadn't forbid it, I thought it best to remain low key, so I returned and sat next to Steve and Betty to await our plane.

When I told Steve that the guards had not recognized *tai chi,* he said that he thought it would make a comeback. Even Buddhism was once again being practiced in China. He had heard that high Communist officials in Beijing regularly attended a Buddhist temple to receive Vajrayana teachings from a Tibetan lama. His prediction did not surprise me, as I remembered from studying history that many cultural practices of conquered peoples are frequently assimilated into the culture of the conquerors. However, the Chinese were still suppressing the free practice of Buddhism in Tibet.[28]

While waiting, I noticed that Betty was still suffering and decided to do the Medicine Buddha practice for her. I turned my attention inward to the Wish-Fulfilling Jewel in my heart, and began the mantra. I imagined that the lapis lazuli body of the God of Healing was seated on a golden throne in the center of a mandala that encompassed the entire airport. Rays of intense blue light radiated into space in every direction. Around him were the Lords of the Four Directions. In the sky above was a ring of ten Archangels, each emitting healing rays. A shaft of blue light shot from the heart of the Medicine to Betty's heart, and I imagined her body filling with blue light. I didn't see immediate results, but knew that as every thought makes an impact, in some way I had helped alleviate her suffering. I also knew that by doing that practice, I had in some irreversible way altered the minds of everyone in the airport.

Suddenly the plane finally arrived and we got Betty on board without incident. However, during the flight

---

[28] The Chinese are presently destroying one of the largest religious institutes in the world, the Buddhist monastery of Larung Gar, which was reported to have a population of 40,000 monks and nuns, many of them Chinese. The Chinese government expressed a plan to reduce the population to 5,000 by the end of September 2017.

she looked as though she were dying. It was a relief when the plane landed in Kathmandu, and the taxi returned us to the Shambhala Hotel. Betty limped to her room, and Steve and I went out to the garden to have tea before saying goodbye.

I thanked him for the expedition and his teachings, especially since the company he worked for had told him to cancel the tour. He confessed that he was quitting the job as guide, since he had not been paid for the last tour, and he doubted they would pay him for this one either. He had paid for our expenses out of his own pocket, hoping for eventual reimbursement.

As we finished our tea, I remembered the Dalai Lama's appearance. I had almost forgotten that he had said he had something for me to do, and asked Steve how he thought I should proceed.

Staring me directly in the eye, he said, "You cannot ignore a request from the Dalai Lama. Go see him in Dharamsala. He will see you, if it is meant to be."

We embraced, and said goodbye. I watched wistfully as this lanky American who had been my companion, guide, and teacher for the past few weeks rose from his seat and strode out of the garden.

I managed to book a flight to Dharamsala that left in two days, so I had a day to explore Kathmandu. But first I wanted to check on Betty, whom I had not seen since she was so deathly ill the day before. I went to her room to find the maid cleaning her empty room, and she had no idea where the occupant had gone. I wondered, had she been taken to the hospital or even died? I went downstairs to inquire.

While waiting at the front desk, a Tibetan girl who worked for the hotel pushed a slip of paper into my hand, and then scurried away. On the note was an address in Kathmandu. Immediately I went outside and climbed in the taxi parked in front of the hotel, and handed the driver the note with the address. Soon, I was deposited before a dilapidated brick house. As though waiting for my arrival, a Tibetan woman came into the street, took me by the hand, and led me into her home. In the back I found Betty sitting up against the wall. She seemed much improved.

She told a remarkable story, that while she was lying in bed, a being made of blue light appeared, and sent a ray of light from his heart to hers. He said that she would be all right and that he would send someone to help her. Then he disappeared. The next morning when the chambermaid came to make up her room and saw how sick she was, she took her home to her family. They said that since she had come so far to visit the Tibetan people, the least they could do was take care of her. They would not accept any money.

"This illness has been a blessing," Betty said. "Even though I teach Sunday school and tell stories about the compassion of Jesus, during my whole life all I have thought about is myself. These people are so kind. When I get back to the States, I am going to try and be more like them. These Tibetans are more Christian than I am."

She then told a remarkable story which started with her childhood. She was the younger of two daughters, and grew up feeling that her father preferred her older sister. No matter what she did to please him, it was never good enough. It wasn't fair, she felt. After the being of blue light disappeared, she dreamed of a past life in which she was a man. She was the father of two daughters, and she preferred the oldest. In this present life, that girl was now her older sister. What she had done in that past life was now what had been done to her in this life.

"It seems that life is fair after all," she said.

"Yes, the realization that we are the creators of our own lives is one of first steps in all spiritual practice," I replied. "Then we can stop blaming life for not being fair, and actually look at what we need to change within ourselves, and by doing that we create a different future."

"You seem to know a lot about these things. Is this what you and Steve were talking about all the time?"

"This and other things."

"Like, what other things?"

"We talked about how the New Age followers have come to believe that the goal is to manipulate life to be more comfortable and to fulfill ones selfish desires, rather than to gain wisdom and compassion.

"Anyway, Betty, it seems that while you were sick you realized the most important things of all, that life is precious and can end at any moment, and that we should make the most of each moment."

"That's for sure," she sighed, "and what comes after that?"

"Well, the last of the main points is the understanding that most suffering comes from the desire for what is not real. Life is impermanent, and all aspects of life are only relatively real and are constantly changing, so grasping for happiness from that *samsara* is bound to lead to suffering. What makes us happy today makes us unhappy tomorrow. My teacher, Pearl, used to tell stories about how half the people who came to her were looking for a relationship, that life would be so much better if they had a partner. The other half of the people complained about being trapped in a relationship, that life would be so much better if they were free. In reality, happiness can only come from within, not from some outer person, place, condition, or thing."

"Oh, speaking of things," Betty said, "I have something I want to give you."

She asked me to get her backpack, as she was still too weak to get up. After rummaging through one of the side pockets, she drew out an object wrapped in a cloth and handed it to me, "Here, I have been feeling bad about taking this, since I think it was meant for you."

I opened the cloth and found that it contained the crystal that the little girl had placed in my hand on the slopes of the mountain below the palace of Yambulagang.

Dalai Lama walking from home to office

Chapter 18

The Dalai Lama's Request

I boarded the plane the next day to Dharamsala to seek out the Dalai Lama. After arriving in town, I got a room at Chonor House, which the guidebooks said afforded a clear view of the Dalai Lama's residence. I wanted to be as close as possible, since I had come specifically to find out what mission he had in mind. Even though he had appeared only on the inner planes, I took this more seriously than if I had received a signed letter. Leaving my bag in the room, I went down to the front porch that overlooked the town and provided a clear view to the opposing hill where the residence was supposed to be located, but saw nothing but an evergreen forest.

When I went to the front desk to inquire about making an appointment for an audience with the Dalai Lama, the clerk broke into a broad grin and laughed, "Do you have some connections? Even when Richard Gere, the Hollywood actor, comes here with an appointment to see His Holiness, sometimes he still has to wait."

Disappointed, I asked for clarification on exactly where His Holiness lived. I heard that he went for a walk around the perimeter of his house every morning, and thought that if I were standing there he would surely stop and talk.

"It's that big yellow building on top of the hill," the clerk said, pointing to the hill at which I had just looked. I was perplexed at not being able to see what he saw, but thanked him and went upstairs to my room to meditate. How was I going to talk to the Dalai Lama if I could not even find his house? I asked my Higher Self to open the way, as I knew that Saint Germain must have a plan and would not have let me come here in vain.

Suddenly I remembered the Precious Wish-Fulfilling Jewel that I had zipped into the pocket inside my backpack. Would it really fulfill wishes? I decided to find out. I found the crumpled slip of paper the doctor had slipped into my hand as we left his office, which explained how to take the pill:

Crush the Most Precious Wish-Fulfilling Jewel the night before, not exposing it to direct light, and dissolve the powder in a mug with a little hot water. Next morning before sunrise, fill the mug with hot water and stir it with the ring finger of your right hand, reciting the Medicine Buddha mantra nine times. Then drink the liquid and go back to bed for an hour, covered by warm blankets. Eliminate from your diet: raw food, onions, garlic, chilies, animal products, and do not engage in sexual activity. To obtain the Precious Wish-Fulfilling Jewel in this life is a rare blessing, and you could only have this opportunity as the result of previous good karma. Do not waste it! In order to ensure the pill's success in transforming all levels of your being, follow these instructions precisely.

Before going to bed, I crushed the marble-like pill into a mug and covered the brown powder with a picture of the Medicine Buddha. If this pill really had the power to grant wishes, what should I ask for? First, I thought of selfish things, like perfect health; but the doctor had already said I was in excellent health. Then, I thought of asking for unlimited wealth so I could serve the Masters without ever worrying about money; but then I realized that I always seemed to have enough money for what I needed. Finally, I realized I needed to ask with a more altruistic motive, and asked for contact with the Dalai Lama, as that seemed to be part of the reason I had been sent here. In conclusion, I asked for the wisdom to benefit others.

I rose at dawn and went down to the dining room and got a thermos of hot water, which I took back to the room. I poured the water over the magical powder and stirred the muddy liquid clockwise with my ring finger as the instructions said. After reciting the Medicine Buddha Mantra, I gulped down the strange tasting liquid just as the sun rose over the hills, then went back to bed. I covered myself with the warm comforter and fell instantly asleep.

I dreamed of Pearl, my former teacher in Mount Shasta, who had left her physical body several years ago. We sat facing each other with eyes open as we often did, meditating on the I AM Presence appearing within each other. As our hearts opened, a radiance flowed between and around us, enveloping us in a mist of light.

Although she did not speak, I heard her inner voice, "Peter, the Wish-Fulfilling Jewel is not an object, but an activity. It is the action of the Mother bringing everything into manifestation—and that you call into action by your intention, thought, love, and spoken word. There is nothing that exists that has not come forth from the Mother, and that creative activity within you is the true Wish-Fulfilling Jewel.

Pearl Dorris, former director of the I AM Sanctuary
of San Francisco

"When your attention is on that Inner Flame, and you say 'I AM,' you call the Wish-Fulfilling Jewel into action," she said, pointing to her heart. "You need only accept it and allow your love to flow into your visualization. Then let go. What your attention is upon, you call into being. Every time you say 'I AM,' you invoke your God Presence into action. Now, use that Jewel to become a Master!"

Gradually Pearl dissolved into light, and I awoke. I sat to meditate, still feeling enveloped by her radiance, and affirmed,

I AM the living light.

As the light grew, I prayed again to know why I been directed here. I affirmed,

I AM the illumining, revealing Presence showing me why I am here.

I AM fulfilling my Divine Mission now.

Suddenly I snapped to attention, remembering that a longtime friend, Kathi Unger, had been sponsoring two sisters at the Tibetan's Children's Village, the Dalai Lama's boarding school up the mountain.[29] She had requested that if I were ever in Dharamsala, to visit the girls, Dechen and Drolma. The strength of the energy I felt seemed to confirm that I should follow through, as it did not seem likely that I was going to see the Dalai Lama any time soon.

I hiked up the path through the woods to the village and went to the administration building, but when I asked for the girls by name there was confusion. Many of the girls had similar names, all of whom were eager for an American visitor. Finally, they found the pair that were sisters, and brought them to the cafeteria

---

[29] To sponsor a child at the Tibetan Children's Village, see their website: www.tcv.org.in.

so we could meet over tea. Wide-eyed, the girls giggled over how much they liked my performance in the film, *Seven Years in Tibet,* the award-winning film about the Austrian, Heinrich Harrer, who escaped from a British prisoner of war camp in India in 1944 to hike into Tibet and become an advisor to the Dalai Lama. They were crestfallen when I told them that the actor had been Brad Pitt. Nor were they impressed when I explained that I had an ancestor who had actually entered Tibet eighty years before Heinrich Harrer.

After some small talk, they showed me around the school. I was appalled that they had no heat. Even in winter, they had to take cold showers and wash their clothes by hand in the icy water from the glaciers. In addition, their meager meals seemed hardly adequate for growing kids. However, the girls were in good spirits. Drolma spoke halting English, but Dechen was fluent and acted as translator.

When I told them that the Dalai Lama had appeared and asked me to do something for him, but I didn't know how to contact him, Dechen said, "Oh, don't worry, my uncle helps the Dalai Lama every day. Maybe he can arrange a meeting! I will tell him you are staying at Chonor House."

I was overjoyed at this surprising turn of events. I might see the Dalai Lama after all! As I prepared to leave, Dechen asked if she could ask me for help with her homework, especially American history. Thinking that I would not hear from her very often, I agreed, and gave her my email address.

By the time I descended the path back to the hotel and consulted my email on the hotel computer, she had already requested assistance. She asked about President

Andrew Jackson, about whom I knew nothing, yet at the end of the email was an electrifying line, "My uncle, Lama Tenzin, will visit you tonight at six pm. He will try to arrange for you to see His Holiness."

Energy began to soar through me. Was it from the prospect of meeting the Dalai Lama, or the delayed effect of the Wish-Fulfilling Jewel? In any case, by evening I was pacing around the hotel. I went out to the porch and looked over the roofs of the town of McLeod Ganj below, then went upstairs to my room to meditate, and then descend again to the porch. Each time I returned to the porch I looked again for the Dalai Lama's residence, where I was sure that I would soon visit, but despite the clear weather there was nothing there.

Finally, I forced myself to sit and still my mind, but the clerk from the front desk appeared and bowed, "Sir, a lama from His Holiness is here. Shall I bring him out?"

"Yes, please," I said, jumping to my feet.

Soon a kindly monk in a maroon robe stood before me, and before I realized what was happening, he bowed and hung a white *kata* (ceremonial silk scarf) around my neck.

"I am Tenzin, Dechen's uncle; so nice to meet you. How do you like the hotel?"

"It's great, except I had expected to see the residence of His Holiness from here."

"Why, it's right there," he said, pointing to the neighboring hill I had been looking at so often.

He was right! There it was. The forest was gone and in its place was a large, light yellow building covering most of the summit. When I explained that I had been unable to see it up until this moment, he explained that the spiritual practice of monks could make it invisible. His presence seemed to allow me to penetrate the veil.

As we watched the sun set, I realized that the hike up the mountain to the school and back had left me famished, and I asked Tenzin if he would join me for dinner. He smiled and said that would be a welcome respite to the bland monastery cuisine.

Over dinner, I mentioned how the Dalai Lama's appearance was the reason for my visit to Dharamsala. Tenzin said that he couldn't promise anything, but would try to arrange a meeting. In the meantime, he offered to give me a tour of the holy sites the next day. He wanted to show me where he taught Buddhist philosophy at the Institute of Buddhist Dialectics, and then continue on to the medical institute. Lastly, he wanted to introduce me to the Venerable Thupten Ngodup, the present Nechung Oracle on whom the Dalai Lama relied to guide the people of Tibet.[30]

That night I had a vivid dream of a past life in Mongolia. I was on a pony, galloping away from a group of invading warriors. My wife sat behind me, her arms encircling my waist. Suddenly she gasped. An arrow had struck her back. Bringing the horse to a standstill, she slumped to the ground. As I plucked out the arrow, she looked up into my eyes, and with her last breath she said, "My love, I'm glad that I could protect you. In a future life find me again." Then she was dead.

---

[30] The Nechung Oracle is the protector spirit that enters the body of the monk, known as the *kuten* (vehicle), who has specifically incarnated for this purpose.

I leapt on my pony and rode like the wind, galloping away across the frozen steppes. I felt hot tears run down my cheeks, and I hoped that I could ride on forever, never stopping.

Awakening with wet cheeks, I knew that Dechen was that girl returned. I had found her, as she had asked. Now I knew why the Dalai Lama had called me here. Even though Dechen was now a young girl of sixteen and I was three times her age, my eternal love for her had lasted through the centuries. I knew that I would do anything for her.

Next morning when her uncle arrived at the hotel, I noticed that the staff bowed with respect. I was touched that this kind-hearted man, who was ordinarily busy helping run the Government of Tibet in Exile, had offered to take me around. As we walked downhill toward lower McLeod Ganj, he explained the difficulty that Tibetan children had in getting college scholarships. All but one or two Indian scholarships went to Indian children, so most of the Tibetan children were unable to attend college.

I kept the revelation about his niece to myself, as I knew it was unwise to talk about inner experiences unless receiving direct guidance to do so. However, as we walked I thought of the College of the Siskiyous, the community college back at the foot of Mount Shasta, which many foreign students attended. Drolma's English was not good enough, but Dechen was fluent and would do fine there.

"Why doesn't Dechen apply to an American college?" I asked. "There is even one near my home."

He stopped in his tracks and looked me straight in the eye, "Would you help her?"

"Sure, I'd be glad to," I said, little dreaming of the complexities that would originate from those few words.

Soon we reached the Institute of Buddhist Dialectics, and he led me inside. Upstairs he showed off a classroom that didn't look much different from any other college classroom, but he surprised me by asking what I studied.

"I study the I AM teachings," I said.

"What's that?"

"The core is that when you say the words 'I AM,' you call your God Self into action."

"Ah yes, the Dharmakaya, but, you can only claim to be one with that aspect of yourself in non-dual awareness. Otherwise you start thinking your personality is God, and you become an egomaniac."

I then remembered a conversation I had in Mount Shasta with the barista at the Seven Suns Cafe. He said he hated the I AM students, because they act so superior. "We all cringe when they come in, because they treat us like dirt."

Pearl also said that she had been glad to escape the I AM Activity for the same reason, that most of the students were what she called "outer," and obsessed with their quest to control everyone and everything, and that because they knew about the Ascended Masters, they were in some way superior to those who did not. She was relieved when years later the "inner" people who practiced meditation began showing up at her door. All she had to do was tell them to turn their attention inward and feel the Presence within their hearts. No amount of affirmations could replace that inner awareness.

"You want to study here?" Tenzin asked, "I could get you in."

"How long a course is it?" I asked, searching my heart if this was a course Saint Germain wanted me to attend.[31]

"Seventeen years," he answered, "but we're now offering shorter courses in English."

"Thanks for the offer," I replied, "but I feel that I am more inclined to learn through meditation."

"Ah, I wish I could meditate," he sighed.

"You don't?" I said, shocked to hear this from a lama.

"No, His Holiness has me so busy running this place and helping out with the government that I hardly get a chance to meditate. Of course, I do get up at four every morning to do prayers along with the rest of the monks."

After we left the Institute of Dialectics, we continued our walk to the medical institute. As we walked in the front door, there again was a thangka of the Medicine Buddha. I had been initiated into the Medicine Buddha practice years before by Master Yu, but had long ago ceased to do it on a regular basis.[32] As

---

[31] The Institute of Buddhist Dialectics in McLeod Ganj now offers online courses in Buddhism in English. See: instituteofbuddhistdialectics.org.

[32] Master Yu Tian Jian (1951-2011), direct disciple of Master Huiling, 48th Maha-Acharya of the Hanmi lineage. This form of esoteric Buddhism is based on Sanskrit texts imported from India into China by the tantric master Subhakarasimha in the year 716 CE.

in all tantric practices, one first enters at least a basic state of samadhi (meditative absorption) in which attachment to the ego ceases. Then one invokes and transforms into the Medicine Buddha. The vows are then said like I AM affirmations, not with the will of the ego, however, but from the truth body of the Higher Self. Tenzin now repeated them for me:

> *I vow that my body shall shine as beams of brilliant light on this infinite and boundless world, showering on all beings, ridding them of ignorance and worries with my teachings.*
> *I vow that I shall grant boundless wisdom to all beings and endow them with all that they require.*
> *I shall relieve them from every kind of illness, pain, suffering, and despair resulting from materialistic desires.*
> *May all beings be like me, the Medicine Buddha, of noble character, with upright mind and soul, and finally attain enlightenment.*

Feeling the power of this vow, I again remembered the vow I had made to Dechen as she lay dying at my feet on the plains of Mongolia. I turned to Tenzin and said, "Yes, of course I will help your niece in whatever way I can."

The next morning, as the sun rose over the hills of McLeod Ganj, I was awakened by a knock at the door. Lama Tenzin walked in, breathless, and blurted out, "I just saw His Holiness, and he said he is very happy you will bring Dechen to America. He gives you his personal blessings!"

I was shocked at this sudden shift. The vague offer I had made had changed overnight into a serious commitment. When I offered help, I envisioned sending her a college application and writing a letter of recommendation, not bringing her to America and taking care of her. I did not even know how I was going to support myself when I returned home, let alone support Dechen; but I had made the commitment and intended to follow through. This is why the Dalai Lama called me here, and for which he had given his blessing.

I wondered what Tenzin had actually said to the Dalai Lama, and how this simple offer had suddenly become a life-changing event. It seemed that any sense of free will was an illusion, that this trip to Tibet and my reunion with Dechen had been determined before our birth. My free will was in choosing to grow from the experiences or not.

Neither of us had eaten breakfast, so we went downstairs to the hotel dining room. He was excited about taking me to meet the Nechung Oracle. I wondered if I could ask him for guidance? However, I sensed Pearl whispering inwardly that I would know intuitively what to do when the time came, and not to look to outer sources that would only weaken my inner strength. By the time we arrived at the Nechung Temple, the oracle had left. Perhaps his absence had saved me from that tendency to give away my power to an external authority. Instead, I contented myself with praying inside before his shrine. I realized that I didn't need clarification. Hadn't I followed my inner guidance to Tibet? Hadn't I discovered the truth of the Wish-Fulfilling Jewel—that it had been in my heart all along? However, I had longed for some enlightened lama to tell me the next part of my mission, how to get Dechen into the United States and what to do with her once she arrived.

I bowed before the shrine, praying to be imparted with some of the omniscience of the Oracle. Going outside, I rejoined Tenzin and thanked him for his kindness. We parted there, vowing to keep in touch, and I walked back to Chonor House. Going online, I managed to find a vacancy on a flight to New Delhi the next day.

Early the next morning, the hotel offered a driver to take me to the airport. I was about to climb into the car, when I saw the hotel manager and the girl from the front desk approaching. The manager bowed with his hands clasped together, and then placed a white *kata* around my neck. The girl did the same, and both said, "Come back again and visit us."

Their sincerity was deeply touching, as though it came not just from two people, but also from the people of Tibet. I had received more than I had anticipated on this trip, more than I could ever have planned by myself. Only by surrendering completely to the I AM Presence could it have unfolded so perfectly. Perhaps I had been using the Most Precious Wish-Fulfilling Jewel all along.

When I returned to Mount Shasta, I began the complex process of helping Dechen get her visa. There were also her college and financial aid applications and endless communications with officials at the Indian consulate, American Embassy in New Delhi, Department of State, Department of Homeland Security, and the United States Customs Service. Fortunately Kathi, Dechen's former sponsor, volunteered to help support her and pay for what was not covered by her scholarship. After a nine-month bureaucratic nightmare, everything was arranged. Dechen would arrive soon. But, where would she stay?

I turned it over to the I AM Presence in meditation, and affirmed,

I AM the Presence bringing Dechen
the perfect place to live.

A week later, I attended Medicine Buddha practice at the home of Chloe, a local lady who frequently sponsored visits to Mount Shasta by the Drepung Monks. When I announced Dechen's arrival, Chloe asked, "Where will she stay?"

"I don't know," I confessed.

"She could stay with me," Chloe volunteered. "I had a dream a week ago, where a Tibetan girl was living with me. I feel that Dechen is her, and I have an extra room."

I drove to the San Francisco airport and met Dechen as she arrived. Exhausted from days of travel, she was grateful to finally have arrived at her destination. Seven hours later, we arrived in Mount Shasta, and I pulled up in front of Chloe's house. She must have been sitting by the door and waiting for us to arrive, for as soon as Dechen got out of the car, Chloe came out to greet her and took Dechen's hands in hers. The two women looked into each other's eyes. Chloe had no children of her own, yet she seemed to have found a daughter. With tears in their eyes, they embraced. I knew that she had found a good home.

Dechen graduated from the junior college with honors and was soon accepted at a nursing school in Ohio, where she had Tibetan friends from childhood. One day as Dechen was preparing to leave, I heard from Chloe that the Nechung Oracle was coming to Mount Shasta to do a ritual, and he would be staying at her house. He would give a blessing Sunday afternoon for anyone who showed up. I thought it strange that I had missed him in Dharamsala, yet he was coming now to where I lived. It seemed that what was meant to be was going to be, with no act of will or attachment to any outcome.

Venerable Thupten Ngodup, the Oracle, conducted the blessing with the assistance of several monks. Since there was not enough room for everyone inside the house, the ceremony was held in the driveway. He gave a preliminary talk during which he stressed the impermanence of all things, including life itself, and stressed that we should regard each moment as precious—and work on liberation so that we could benefit others.

When he concluded, everyone formed a line and filed up one by one to receive his blessing. I was the last in line, and when I stood before him, the Oracle stopped. He looked me in the eye and asked, "What are you doing here?"

"What do you mean?" I asked.

"What are you *doing* here?" he repeated.

"I live here," I explained.

He smiled, then picked up the metal statue of Chenrezig, the Lord of Compassion, and brought it down on my head with a thud. I walked away, wondering why he had asked that. I looked up and saw a rainbow overhead, and realized that the Oracle did not want an answer. It was a question I needed to answer myself. *What am I doing here?*

Dechen was standing shyly at the edge of the driveway under a tree, and I went to her and asked, "Why did he use the statue of Chenrezig to bless me?"

"Because he transmits the compassionate aspect of Mahakala."[33]

"What, I thought that Mahakala was always black and wrathful?"

---

[33] Mahakala is an aspect of consciousness that can appear in various manifestations, depending on the intent of the invocation. Over time many of the aspects changed, depending on the intent and lineage of the practitioner. The demon that Padmasambhava subdued at Samye Monastery was known as Pehar, a powerful demon from a class of beings known as a *Gyalpos*. These demons could appear in any form they wished, including the black Mahakala. These are considered to be the souls of kings and spiritual practitioners who broke their vows and turned against the dharma to pursue egoistic goals. They are said to frequently re-embody on Earth as rulers or spiritual teachers whose emphasis is mainly on the acquisition of wealth, power, and fame. They may also embody as rulers, rock stars, and other fame seekers. Today it is possible that many world leaders and public figures are of this class of demons, or are influenced by them.

"Oh no, there is a white form also that bestows abundance and compassion. The white form of Mahakala is called *Chintamani,* the Wish-Fulfilling Jewel. Within yourself is the black form as well as the white form. It is their job to help you cut through illusion, and to see if you will ask for material things or spiritual wealth in the form of the enlightened heart of the compassionate Buddha."[34]

As I looked at her in surprise, I saw for a second the Mongolian girl who had been my wife so long ago. I wanted to say something, but my heart was so full I could not speak. Then, she turned and went inside the house. It was the last time I would see her, as she left the next day for Ohio.

I had frequently wanted to discuss our past life together, but the time had never seemed appropriate. The Masters always said to keep inner revelations to yourself, unless prompted otherwise. Now that she was gone, I felt the same loss as when she lay dying at my feet on the plains of Mongolia. I wanted her to come back outside so that I could express what was in my heart, but turned instead and walked down the driveway.

A year later, on the Tibetan New Year, I received an unexpected card from Dechen. On the outside was the White Tara. Inside she wrote:

---

[34] *Chintamani* is another name for the *Rinchen Ratna Samphel,* the Most Precious Wish-Fulfilling Jewel. In western esotericism, it is known as the Philosopher's Stone. Possession of this jewel opens one to the compassionate wisdom of the Buddhas.

Dear Peter,

I wanted to let you know how well I am doing. I am going to nursing school so that I can someday help others. I want to thank you for making the effort to bring me to America. I know you had to go through a lot for me, but you have given me a life I would never have had otherwise. Thank you from the bottom of my heart. I will always love you.

Your friend,
Dechen

Chapter19

Chenrezig - Lord of Compassion

I sat on the sofa in my living room, rereading Dechen's letter. Once again, my heart opened and I felt the love I had felt long ago. Instead of grasping and feeling once more that pain, I decided to transmute that longing.

I was aware of my breathing, and focused on the in breath and out breath, allowing my mind to slow and relax, so that all I could feel was the pain in my heart like a dark void. I thought *how many others there must be at this very moment feeling the same pain,* and saw that I was in the center of a vast mandala filled with those countless people.

I began the mantra,

Om Mani Padme Hung

Suddenly, before me arose the vision of Dechen, looking at me with great concern, "What is it you want, Peter?" I heard her ask inwardly.

"I just wanted to tell you how much I love you. During your time here, it never seemed right to say that."

"I know, but I felt it anyway."

"You did?"

"Of course," she replied, "and I also wanted to thank you for finding me again, for giving me a new start in this life. Perhaps in some future life we will meet again."

For a moment, we looked into each other's eyes with our hearts fully open, and a beam of light passed between us. Dechen became more and more luminous, gradually transforming into Chenrezig, the Lord of Compassion.

Seated within a pink lotus, a golden letter Hung appeared in the center of her chest, which began to glow with golden light. As a ray of that light penetrated my heart— suddenly, I was Chenrezig, sitting in the lotus—and I realized,

I am Dechen...I am Chenrezig...
I am the Lord of Compassion.

Chenrezig, Lord of Compassion

From the golden sun that now filled my heart, thousands of rays of light emanated into space, a ray entering the heart of each of the souls seated in my mandala. As each absorbed this ray of love, the darkness within disappeared and a smile appeared on each face. There were Karma and Lobsang in front, radiant in their higher bodies, and I let go of the pain I felt over their suffering. I saw that they had fulfilled their karmic lessons and were liberated. Gradually everything disappeared, all sense of self and other. There was only compassion emanating into space—the Wish-Fulfilling Jewel in my heart.

Ascended Master Saint Germain